GETTING ORGANIZED
FOR YOUR NEW BABY

by Maureen Bard

Meadowbrook

Distributed by Simon and Schuster
New York

Dedication

To our daughter, Sara

Library of Congress Cataloging in Publication Data

Bard, Maureen
  Getting organized for your new baby.

  Bibliography: p.116
  1. Pregnancy—Forms. 2. Childbirth—Forms.
3. Infants—Care and hygiene—Forms. 1. Title.
RG525.B266 1986   618.2   86-8485
ISBN 0-88166-081-7

S&S Ordering #: 0-671-62275-7 (priced)

Art Direction: Nancy MacLean
Editorial: Jean D'Alessio, Chris Larsen, Catherine Ballman
Cover Design: Nancy MacLean, Mary Foster
Text Design: Mary Foster
Keyline: Mike Tuminelly
Production: John Howard

Contents

Chapter Three: Mother's Needs

Chapter Four: Baby's Needs

Chapter Five: Family Members and Household Needs

Chapter Six: Financial Planning

Chapter Seven: Celebrations

Chapter Eight: Day Care and Babysitters

Chapter Nine: Final Countdown

Resources

INTRODUCTION

You know you're pregnant when you start buying baby books to help you sort out all the questions you have about pregnancy and birth. Should I change my eating habits? Where do I find the best doctor? What clothes and furniture will my baby need? How will we manage our finances with a new baby? What do I take to the hospital?

Pregnancy can be overwhelming, especially for the first-time mother. I know. I've been there, and so have the parents I surveyed when researching this book. I asked them what information would help them "get organized" for a new baby—their answers are the basis for what follows.

But, *Getting Organized For Your New Baby* doesn't just tell you how to get organized, it involves you in the process. Over seventy-five charts and checklists provide a step-by-step guide, helping you plan the many details so you can truly enjoy this wonderful and very exciting time of your life.

Getting Organized For Your New Baby is a practical, easy-to-use guide that takes you from your first days of pregnancy through the trip to the hospital and back home again. It offers tips on nutrition, morning sickness and exercise. It suggests ways to find an obstetrician and a pediatrician and discusses birth plans. Clothing needs for mother and baby are detailed, plus nursery decorating tips and equipment. The important area of organizing your household for a new baby—including your finances—is covered, as well as child care options, celebrations and much more.

So sit down and put your feet up, grab your pencil, and let's get organized!

Maureen Bard

Chapter One
Your Body Is Changing!

Nutrition

A balanced diet during pregnancy is essential for both you and your developing baby. The foods you eat must support the additional demands of the fetus, placenta, membranes, increased maternal blood volume and breast development. (See Nutrition and Vitamin chart in the Appendix.) The following materials can be used to evaluate your diet and record your weight gain.

Basic Dietary Considerations During Pregnancy

Food Group	Examples	Recommended Amounts*
Dairy products	Milk, yogurt, ice cream, cheese	3-4 servings daily
High protein	Meat, fish, poultry	3-4 servings daily
Green, yellow vegetables	Spinach, broccoli, squash, carrots	1-2 servings daily
Citrus fruits	Citrus juice, oranges, grapefruit	2 servings daily
Other vegetables, fruits	Potatoes, beets, cauliflower, peaches, apples	1 serving daily
Bread, flour, cereals	Bread, macaroni, cereals, muffins	2-4 servings daily
Fats, oils	Margarine, butter	1-2 servings daily
Fluids	Water, milk	8+ servings daily
Sugar foods	Sugar, candy, honey, jam, chocolate	0 servings

*Recommended amounts vary depending upon the pregnancy and mother's appetite.

Mother's Diet Worksheet

Use this worksheet to evaluate your daily diet. If you are consistently deficient in a food group you might want to contact a nutritionist, dietician or physician for recommendations.

Date: _____ Week of Pregnancy: _____

Food Group	Servings	When Consumed	Calories	Total No. Servings	Evaluation**
Dairy Products (3 to 4 servings)					
High Protein (3 to 4 servings)					
Green, yellow vegetables (1-2 servings)					
Citrus fruits (2 servings)					
Other vegetables, fruits (1 serving)					
Bread, flour, cereals (2 to 4 servings)					
Fats, oils (1 to 2 servings)					
Fluids (8+ servings)					
Sugary foods (0 servings)					

Total + = _____
Total − = _____

*Use the following code:
  B - breakfast, L - lunch, D - dinner, S - snack.
**Use a "+" when the minimum recommendation has been met and a "−" when a deficiency occurs. Exclude sugary foods from the evaluation of nutrients.

Evaluation:

8 or more +: "Way to go, Mom! Thanks!"
8 or more −: "Mom, I'm not on a diet down here!"

Note: Pregnant women should consume between 2,100 and 2,400 calories daily.

Plotting Your Pregnancy Weight Gain

Monitor your weight gain by completing the following graph:

Step 1: Current weight   _____
         Minus prepregnant weight   _____
         Pounds gained   _____

Step 2: Find the pounds gained number on the vertical axis of the graph.

Step 3: Find the week of your pregnancy on the horizontal axis.

Step 4: Plot your weight gain by finding the point on the graph where your pounds gained intersects with the week of your pregnancy.

Step 5: Connect the dot from the previous week to form a continuous line.

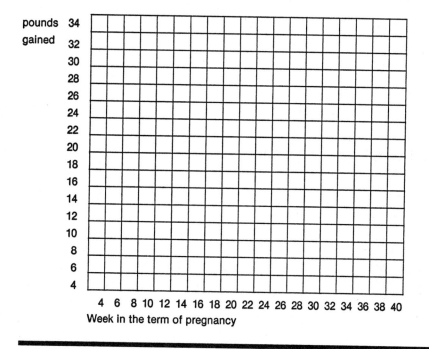

A graphic reminder of your changing shape is fun to have. Post a picture of your pre-pregnant self, with the date the photo was taken, on the next page. When you're close to your due date, have your husband or a friend take a picture of you. You'll be amazed at the difference nine months makes!

4

Prepregnancy Photograph
Date taken: _____

Photograph Taken Near Due Date
Date taken: _____

Morning Sickness and Constipation

The first falsehood of pregnancy—if you get past the morning you won't suffer morning sickness—is not true. Morning sickness can occur any time of the day or night. It is very individualized as are the successes or failures of the remedies.

Morning Sickness Survival Kit

Carry the following with you at all times:

Snacks	High protein (peanuts) High in carbohydrates (saltine crackers)
Hard candy	Sucking on hard candy or lollipops sometimes helps.
Moist towelettes Breath mints	Help refresh after a bout of nausea.
Fan	Helps if you feel suffocated by still air or crowds of people.
Small plastic bag	To carry all of the above; use the bag in an emergency as a "motion sickness" bag.

Morning Sickness Remedies

Never allow your stomach to become empty, your blood sugar level to drop or stomach acid to accumulate. Keep track of remedies below:

Suggestions	Tried	Helped	No Relief
Diet considerations:			
Eat 5 to 6 small meals.	☐	☐	☐
Increase protein intake.	☐	☐	☐
Eat soda crackers or dry toast.	☐	☐	☐
Increase foods rich in vitamin B6.	☐	☐	☐
Avoid greasy or spicy foods.	☐	☐	☐
Fluid intake considerations:			
Drink liquids throughout the day.	☐	☐	☐
Avoid drinking liquids with meals.	☐	☐	☐
Avoid caffeine and herbal teas with aloe, buckhorn bark, duck roots, juniper berries and senna leaves.	☐	☐	☐
Drink herbal teas with chamomile, peach leaf, peppermint and spearmint.	☐	☐	☐
Drink liquids very hot or very cold.	☐	☐	☐
Drink acidic fruit juices on full stomach.	☐	☐	☐

Morning Sickness Routine

The morning sickness routine actually begins before going to bed. If you are particularly susceptible to morning nausea, try the following:

The night before: Place crackers or toast on bedstand. Set alarm clock 20 minutes earlier to avoid rushing. Place face cloth in a bowl of water on bedstand.

In the morning: Eat crackers or toast 20 minutes before getting out of bed. Place damp face cloth over eyes. Go for a morning walk or get fresh air through an open window. Minimize odors which may cause nausea such as coffee brewing, perfume, aftershave or scented toiletries.

Constipation Remedies

Constipation is caused by the slowing of your digestive system. The following suggestions might help:

Suggestion	Tried	Helped	No Relief
Exercise.	☐	☐	☐
Drink plenty of fluids.	☐	☐	☐
Eat high-fiber foods:			
dried fruits	☐	☐	☐
raw vegetables	☐	☐	☐
whole grains	☐	☐	☐
prune juice	☐	☐	☐
Eat fruits with known laxative qualities:			
prunes	☐	☐	☐
figs	☐	☐	☐
dates	☐	☐	☐
raisins	☐	☐	☐
apples	☐	☐	☐

Fatigue

Fatigue is generally associated with the first trimester of pregnancy. You may become faint, exhausted or irritable. Because your body requires more rest, consider some of these strategies.

- Take Quick Naps

  Try napping while children are at school, napping or visiting friends, during coffee breaks and lunch breaks, or when you come home from work before dinner. If you nap at work, be sure to use a timer or a watch with an alarm to avoid oversleeping. Look for quiet spaces at work such as a lounge, an extra office, or your own office with a sign on the door which reads, "I'm on the phone. Please do not disturb."

- Learn to Say "No."

  Now is the time to limit your involvement in clubs and other activities which require your time and energy.

- Discuss with your supervisor the possibility of flexible (flex) time. The arrangement could include the following:

  Taking work home.

  Coming into the office on weekends to "catch up" on projects.

  Sharing your job with a co-worker.

  Working a shorter day and keeping track of the abbreviated hours (see card below). When 8 hours of work have been missed, your supervisor can deduct one sick day.

Flexible Time Card

Date	Time I Came In	Time I Left	Standard Starting Time	Standard Quitting Time	Hours Short

Daily Routine Scheduler

To complete this form, rate your personal energy level at each hour of the day on a scale of 1 to 4 (1 when your energy level is high; 4 when you are very fatigued), and record in Column 1.

Then list all the tasks which take concentration and high levels of energy, as well as those which require less concentration and energy. Evaluate the activity using the number 1 for those needing high energy and concentration, 2 for those needing less energy and concentration and so on. For example:

handle correspondence (1)   dust (3)
make beds (2)   address envelopes (4)

Organize your day by combining the information in Column 1 of the chart with your list of activities. Place the tasks which require less energy and concentration in the low-energy time slots. Some tasks must be accomplished at certain times regardless of your fatigue level, but you might minimize the fatigue by planning low-energy activities before and after those tasks.

Time	Column 1 Energy Level: 1 to 4 (1 = high, 4 = fatigued)	Column 2 (1 = requiring high energy, 4 = requiring low energy)
midnight-1 a.m.		
1-2 a.m.		
2-3 a.m.		
3-4 a.m.		
4-5 a.m.		
5-6 a.m.		
6-7 a.m.		
7-8 a.m.		
8-9 a.m.		
9-10 a.m.		
10-11 a.m.		
11 a.m.-noon		
noon-1 p.m.		
1-2 p.m.		
2-3 p.m.		
3-4 p.m.		
4-5 p.m.		
5-6 p.m.		
6-7 p.m.		
7-8 p.m.		
8-9 p.m.		
9-10 p.m.		
10-11 p.m.		
11 p.m.-midnight		

Prohibitions During Pregnancy

Pregnancy comes with its own list of things to avoid. Basically, they can be divided into nutritional, medicinal and environmental considerations. The following chart lists some of these prohibitions with alternative suggestions.

Prohibition List

Items To Avoid	Alternatives
Medicinal	
X-rays (dental & medical)	
Analgesics, aspirin	Warm, relaxing bath with massage
	Tension-reducing exercises
	Hot packs on neck and shoulders, cold pack on forehead
Cold, cough medications	Cool mist vaporizer
	Lemon and honey
	Rest
Muscle relaxants for backache	Massage
	Hot and cold packs
	Warm shower with hand-held shower nozzle pointed on the ache
	Exercise
Sleeping pills	Brisk walk
	Warm bath or shower
	Reading material
	Massage, soothing music
Environmental	
Smoking	Avoid smoke-filled rooms.
	Inform smokers of your concerns.
Toxic chemicals: lacquer thinner fumes volatile paints oven cleaner	Use latex paint—preferably when you are absent.
	Allow fumes to dissipate.
	Hire out heavy cleaning involving harsh chemicals.
Pesticides	Use mechanical items such as bug zappers instead of chemicals.
Herbicides	Do not hang wallpaper, as many are treated with herbicides.
	Inform your company's maintenance department that you wish to be notified before they spray.
Cat litter and unknown cats (due to danger of toxoplasmosis from cats that eat infected meat)	Keep cat indoors.
	Feed cat commercially prepared foods.
	Have someone else change cat litter box.

Nutritional

Raw or uncooked meat (danger of toxoplasmosis)	Cook to internal temperature of at least 140 degrees
Alcohol	Try soft drinks or mixed drinks without the alcohol (i.e. Virgin Marys).
Caffeine	Drink decaffeinated or caffeine-free beverages. Reduce caffeine in tea by limiting steeping time and not boiling the water.
Food additives: BHA, BHT, sodium nitrates, sodium nitrites (found in cured, preserved and smoked foods such as bacon, ham, luncheon meats)	Eat unprocessed foods. Read labels carefully.
Saccharin (crosses the placental barrier)	Use real sugar where necessary in limited amounts.

The most important thing to remember is to err on the side of caution. If you have any questions about the safety of a substance, do not ingest or use it. A quick call to your physician or other health care provider will establish whether or not a substance is safe for you and your baby.

Classes and Exercise

Some women enjoy enrolling in classes during pregnancy. Exercise sessions, educational programs and childbirth classes provide you with stimulation and much-needed information and techniques. But more importantly, the class membership provides you with an automatic comparison of belly sizes. Consider the following checklist of popular classes, workshops and seminars.

Prenatal Class Schedule

	To Check On	Enrolled	Schedule (Trimester)
Educational			
Prenatal nutrition classes	☐	☐	☐
Childbirth preparation classes	☐	☐	☐
Cesarean preparation classes	☐	☐	☐
Breastfeeding classes	☐	☐	☐
Baby care classes	☐	☐	☐
First aid classes	☐	☐	☐
Special classes and organizations for high-risk pregnancies, children with genetic abnormalities, premature and multiple births.	☐	☐	☐
Exercise and fitness			
Pregnancy exercise classes	☐	☐	☐
Organized activities for pregnant women such as swimming laps, walking and bicycle groups	☐	☐	☐
Postpartum exercise classes	☐	☐	☐
Exercise, massage classes for the newborn	☐	☐	☐

Class sponsors

YMCA/YWCA
Hospital education departments
Health maintenance organizations
Physicians' groups
County health departments
Women's groups
Colleges, universities
Special organizations, interest groups (Check the national headquarters for the address of your local chapter.)

Prenatal Class Evaluator

Use the following evaluator to check out classes offered in your area. Content and instructors vary widely so be sure you know what you're getting before you sign up.

Class name _____ Instructor's name _____

	Good	Fair	Poor
Instructor's qualifications			
Experience in labor and delivery	☐	☐	☐
Experience as mother or grandmother	☐	☐	☐
Formal education	☐	☐	☐
Continued professional development: in-service workshops, courses, seminars attended:			
_____			
_____			
_____	☐	☐	☐
Enthusiasm and open-mindedness	☐	☐	☐
Knowledge of community resources	☐	☐	☐
Course outline			
Prenatal exercise and nutrition	☐	☐	☐
Pregnancy physiology	☐	☐	☐
Stages of labor/discussion of expectations	☐	☐	☐
Relaxation techniques/instructional and practice time	☐	☐	☐
Orientation to the hospital/clinic, including hands-on familiarization with equipment such as infant monitors, amniotic hook, I.V.'s, catheters	☐	☐	☐
Care of the newborn	☐	☐	☐
Apgar scoring	☐	☐	☐
Hospital routine immediately after birth, including bonding time, separation from mother, immediate care of newborn in nursery (i.e. heat light, warming table), extent of special-care nursery facilities.	☐	☐	☐
Instruction in the general care of a newborn: bathing, feeding, bonding, diapering.	☐	☐	☐

Chapter Two
Choosing Doctors and Birth Plans

Finding a Doctor

Often, former maternity patients have very positive or very negative feelings toward their obstetrical caregivers. You'll hear comments like "fantastic, supportive, caring" or "I'd run that jerk down in a crosswalk!" Interview and evaluate your caregiver carefully.

Resources

Possible places where you might locate an obstetrical caregiver include:

- Labor/delivery or birthing center of the hospital/clinic. Phone the hospital or clinic where you wish to deliver. Explain your Birth Plan to the labor/delivery room nurse and ask for suggestions. Hospital staff see the caregivers in action and, therefore, are able to evaluate their performance.

- Friends with children. Former maternity patients usually have strong feelings toward their caregivers. Take both their positive and negative comments into consideration.

- County health association or board of health
- American Red Cross
- Family practitioner or family physician
- State licensing agencies
- American Medical Association local chapter
- Mothers in childbirth classes
- Instructors in childbirth classes
- Teaching hospitals
- Health maintenance organizations

Someone once said the three most important questions to ask an obstetrician were: 1) Do you take vacations? 2) Do you participate in any underwater sports which make you unable to hear a beeper? 3) Do you live within walking distance of the hospital?

Selecting a caregiver with whom you feel comfortable is crucial to a successful birthing experience. Too often, the caregiver is selected first and the expectant parents conform to his or her philosophy. To avoid this situation:

• Familiarize yourself with the birthing options in your community.
• Formulate a Birth Plan.

Birth Plan Options

The following is a list of common practices in labor, birth, and postpartum, along with options for handling each. Discuss the options with your childbirth educator and caregiver, and take tours of local hospitals to discover what you want. Then make up a rough draft of your Birth Plan. Go over it with your caregiver and make a final draft. Make several copies—one to keep, one for your medical chart, and one for your baby's chart.

Procedure or Practice	Options
During labor	
Enema	☐ No enema
	☐ Self-administered at home
	☐ Administered in hospital
	☐ Oil retention or water enema
Prep (shaving of pubic hair)	☐ No removal of pubic hair
	☐ Clip hair around vagina
	☐ Shave hair around vagina
	☐ Shave all pubic hair
Presence of partner	☐ Mother's choice
	☐ One or more partners present throughout labor and birth
	☐ At doctor's, nurse's or anesthesiologist's discretion
Position for labor	☐ Freedom to change position and walk around
	☐ Confined to bed in various positions
	☐ Confined to one position in bed
Onset of labor	☐ Spontaneous (begins on its own)
	☐ Self-induced: nipple stimulation, enema, castor oil
	☐ Induced after fetal maturity studies for medical reasons
	☐ Medical or surgical induction: artificial rupture of the membranes, prostaglandin gel, intravenous pitocin
	☐ Induced without fetal maturity studies
Hydration/fluids	☐ Popsicles
	☐ Water, juice
	☐ I.V. fluids
	☐ Ice chips only
	☐ No liquids

Vaginal exams	☐ At mother's request
	☐ Only when labor changes
	☐ Occasionally
	☐ Frequent
Monitoring fetal heart	☐ Auscultation with stethoscope
	☐ Auscultation with Doptone
	☐ Intermittent external electronic fetal monitoring
	☐ Internal electronic fetal monitoring for medical reasons
	☐ Routine continuous electronic monitoring—internal or external
Pain relief	☐ Relaxation, breathing, comfort measures
	☐ Medications, anesthesia only at mother's request
	☐ Medications routine
Enhance or speed labor	☐ Walk, change position
	☐ Nipple stimulation
	☐ Enema
	☐ Rupture of membranes
	☐ Pitocin
To empty bladder	☐ Walk to toilet
	☐ Bedside commode
	☐ Bedpan in bed
	☐ Catheterization

During birth

Position	☐ Choice of position
	☐ Use of stirrups
Expulsion techniques	☐ Spontaneous, short bearing-down
	☐ Directed pushing
	☐ Prolonged pushing
Speed-up birth	☐ Gravity-enhancing positions
	☐ Prolonged pushing on command
	☐ Episiotomy
	☐ Forceps or vacuum extractor
Bed for birth	☐ Mother's choice of birth chair, bean bag, floor, bed
	☐ Birthing bed
	☐ Labor bed
	☐ Delivery table with stirrups
Cleanliness of perineum	☐ Undraped, mother touches baby during birth
	☐ Sterile, with drapes, masks, etc.
Care of perineum	☐ Try for intact perineum with massage, support, hot compresses.
	☐ Anesthesia, episiotomy, stitches
	☐ Ice packs immediately after birth

After birth

Delivery of placenta	☐ Spontaneous
	☐ Encouraged with breast stimulation, baby suckling
	☐ Hastened with massage of the fundus, pitocin
	☐ Manual extraction
Cord cutting	☐ Father cuts cord
	☐ Clamp and cut after it stops pulsating
	☐ Clamp and cut immediately

Baby care

Airway	☐ Baby coughs and expels own mucus, suctioned if necessary
	☐ Suction almost immediately
	☐ Deep suctioning
Warmth	☐ Baby skin-to-skin with mother, with blanket covering both
	☐ Wrapped in heated blanket
	☐ Placed in thermostatically-controlled, heated isolette
Immediate care	☐ Baby held by parents and suckled by mother
	☐ Kept near parents in bassinet or isolette
	☐ Taken to nursery for observation, weighing, feeding
Eye care	☐ None
	☐ Nonirritating agent, such as erythromycin or tetracycline, within 1 hour
	☐ Silver nitrate, within 1 hour
	☐ Silver nitrate immediately
First feedings	☐ Breastfeeding on demand
	☐ Scheduled breastfeeding
	☐ Water, by medicine dropper or bottle, given by parents or nurse
	☐ Glucose water
	☐ Formula feedings on demand
	☐ Scheduled formula feedings
Contact with baby	☐ 24-hour rooming-in
	☐ Daytime rooming-in
	☐ For feedings only, in nursery at other times
Circumcision	☐ None
	☐ With parents present to comfort baby
	☐ With no anesthesia
	☐ With anesthesia
	☐ Out-of-hospital circumcision
Discharge of mother and baby	☐ When desired
	☐ Within 6 to 12 hours of birth
	☐ 3 or more days after birth

Obstetrical Caregiver Evaluator

As you interview the caregiver, evaluate him or her on the basis of your needs. Ask additional questions such as: Why has the caregiver taken this position or attitude? How flexible is the caregiver to change?

The checklist below will help you evaluate a caregiver. Take the birthing plan outline from the preceding pages which you just filled out with you to the interview. Ask the physician or midwife about each of the points and record the response.

Name: _____   Telephone Number: _____
                                   Appointment Date: _____

Accessibility and personal care

Procedure for telephoned-in questions   _____

Amount of physician/patient contact
time during prenatal examinations,
labor, delivery, postpartum (hospital and
at home)   _____

Role of associates/partners/office
personnel   _____

Individual vs. group practice   _____

Number of professionals in the group   _____

Examinations:

   Who will I see?   _____

   How frequently?   _____

   His or her responsibility?   _____

Actual birth:

   Probability of another person delivering?   _____

   Who is back-up if an emergency occurs?   _____

Affiliations

Is there a choice of hospital?   _____

Prenatal care

Frequency of appointments   _____

Attitude toward visitors during
appointments:

   Siblings   _____

   Birthing Coach   _____

   Other family members   _____

Recommendations for:

   Childbirth classes   _____

   Literature and resource materials   _____

   Support groups   _____

   Exercise classes   _____

Procedures or practices during labor

Enema and prep _____
Presence of partner(s), family members _____
Position for labor _____
Hydration fluids _____
Vaginal exams _____
Monitoring fetal heart _____
Pain relief _____
Enhance or speed labor _____
Emptying bladder _____

Procedures and practices during birth

Position _____
Expulsion techniques _____
Speed-up birth _____
Bed for birth _____
Cleanliness of perineum _____
Care of perineum _____

Postpartum

Phone-in hours _____
Appointments _____
Frequency of examination _____

Office procedures

Fees _____
Will my insurance cover costs? _____
Who will do the paperwork? _____
Average waiting time for my
appointment _____
Will office contact me if appointments
are running late? _____
Accessibility to:
  Workplace _____
  Babysitter _____
Comfort of the office environment:
  Waiting area _____
  Examination rooms _____

The Unexpected

If problems develop either during labor or afterwards, you may have to relinquish some of your desired options, and more interventions may be necessary for safety. The following are some options that are usually available even under such circumstances.

Procedure or Practice	Options

Cesarean birth

Timing (if cesarean is planned)	☐ After labor begins
	☐ Scheduled before labor begins
Partner's presence	☐ Father or partner present
	☐ No partner present
Anesthesia	☐ Regional with little or no premedication
	☐ Regional anesthesia with premedication
	☐ General anesthesia
Participation	☐ Screen lowered at time baby is delivered
	☐ Anesthesiologist or obstetrician explains events
	☐ No explanation to parents
Contact with baby	☐ Held by father soon after birth, where mother can touch and see
	☐ Breastfeeding as soon as possible
	☐ Sent immediately to nursery or intensive care
Discharge	☐ Less than 5 days
	☐ 5 days or more

Premature or sick infant

Contact with baby	☐ Parents visit and care for baby as much as possible.
	☐ If baby is in another hospital from mother, father goes with baby
	☐ Baby separated from parents with little or no visiting
Feeding when baby is able to digest food. (Before this point, the baby is fed intravenously.)	☐ Mother nurses baby
	☐ Mother's expressed milk to be given to baby by bottle, dropper or tube
	☐ Formula feeding by bottle, dropper or tube
	☐ Fed by parents or nurse
Contact with support group	☐ Initiated by parents, nurses or support group
	☐ No contact

Prenatal Visits

Keeping track of your prenatal visits can be very interesting. Your body is changing rapidly and the baby's developmental stages are fascinating to record. This information also can be very useful in subsequent pregnancies, especially if you change caregivers.

Initially you will be asked for a medical history. Review the following with your husband. This is particularly important if your husband will not be attending the first prenatal appointment.

Medical History Organizer

Present medical history of mother

Problem	Yes	No	Week of Pregnancy
Nausea	☐	☐	_____
Vomiting	☐	☐	_____
Fatigue	☐	☐	_____
Headache	☐	☐	_____
Visual problems	☐	☐	_____
Edema (water retention)	☐	☐	_____
Urinary problems	☐	☐	_____
Constipation	☐	☐	_____
Bleeding	☐	☐	_____
Anemia	☐	☐	_____

Past medical history of mother

Date of last period: _____ Duration: _____

Cycle: _____

Method of birth control: _____

Menarche (your age when you began menstruating): _____

Other pregnancies:

number: _____

dates: _____

term: _____

problems: _____

_____

List of childhood diseases: _____

Hospitalization dates: _____

   Did you receive transfusions? _____

   Did you undergo any operations? _____

Family medical history

Problem	Grand-parents	Mother	Father	Sibling	Sibling
Allergies	☐	☐	☐	☐	☐
Diabetes	☐	☐	☐	☐	☐
Hypertension	☐	☐	☐	☐	☐
Heart disease	☐	☐	☐	☐	☐
Congenital disorders	☐	☐	☐	☐	☐
Multiple births	☐	☐			
Stillbirths	☐	☐			

Comments _____

_____

_____

_____

_____

_____

_____

_____

_____

_____

_____

_____

_____

_____

_____

_____

_____

_____

_____

_____

Obstetrical Record and Calendar

The form which follows will help you record the progress of your pregnancy. Measurement refers to the height of the maternal fundus; the caregiver will be measuring the top of the uterus from your pelvic bone. This measurement is used to monitor the baby's growth.

Week of Pregnancy	Date Appt.	Weight	Blood Pressure	Pulse	Measurement	Heart Rate
0-4						
4-8						
8-12						
12-14						
14-16						
16-18						
18-20						
20-22						
22-24						
25						
26						
27						
28						
29						
30						
31						
32						
33						
34						
35						
36						
37						
38						
39						
40						

Week-to-Week Observations

Week of Pregnancy	Maternal Changes	Fetal Development	Questions/ Comments
0-4	May be nauseated, faint or tired	Forming umbilical cord, spine, simple heart	_____
4-8	Increased vaginal secretions	Forming face, arms, legs, tooth buds	_____
8-12	Frequent urination; fuller breasts	Arms, legs move, can smile, frown	_____
12-14	Fetal movement noticeable	Strong heartbeat, active muscles	_____
14-16	May have food cravings	Skin is transparent, downy hair (lanugo)	_____
16-18	May be constipated; uterus top at navel	Heartbeat is audible, sucks thumb	_____
18-20	Relaxing pelvic joints	Hiccups; hair, eyelashes formed	_____
20-22	May have leg cramps; gums may bleed	Wrinkled skin, eyes are open	_____
22-24	Uterus above navel; voice may change	Meconium in bowel, strong grip	_____
25-28	May have backache, heartburn, anemia, varicose veins, insomnia	14-17 inches long, adding body fat, very active, basic breathing movements	_____
29-32	May have shortness of breath, hemorrhoids, swollen ankles	16½–18 inches long, sleep and active periods, responds to sounds, liver stores iron	_____
33-36	May have stretch marks; urination & perspiration increases	19 inches long, weighs 6 pounds, skin less wrinkled, less active, gaining immunities	_____
37-40	Braxton-Hicks increased energy contractions, bloody show	20 inches long, 7 pounds, fat body, mature lungs, arms, legs are flexed	_____

Breast vs. Bottle

In recent years, breastfeeding has had a rebirth. Both your obstetrical caregiver and your baby's physician are interested in your decision to breast or bottle feed. The obstetrical caregiver will advise you concerning the preparation of your breasts if you choose to breastfeed. The baby's caregiver will be interested in this information for his or her records.

Breastfeeding Pros and Cons

Pros

Nutritionally the best

Easier for baby to digest

Convenient once the routine has been established

Increases maternal weight loss

Enhances bonding

Increased protection for baby against infection and disease

Costs (cheaper than the expense of bottles, nipples, formula)

Cons

More time-consuming because nursing babies nurse more frequently

Mother more confined—must be there to feed baby until enough milk can be expressed

Maternal medical problems (cracked nipples)

Concern if mother is on medication

Maternal attitude (Some women find it distasteful or uncomfortable)

Bottle Feeding Considerations

Formula

Formula comes in several different forms and many different compositions. Discuss with your baby's caregiver which formula he or she wants you to give the baby.

Type of Formula	Features
Prepackaged	The formula is mixed and in a disposable bottle and nipple. This is the most expensive formula but also the most convenient.
Canned premixed	The formula is mixed and all you do is pour it into the bottles.
Powdered	You must mix the powder with water. An advantage over the concentrated liquid is that you can make up small quantities at a time, i.e. one bottle.
Concentrated liquid	You must dilute the liquid formula with water and pour into the bottles.

Materials

Decide which type of bottle works best for you and your budget.

Type	Requirements
Disposable bottles	Nipples
	Plastic bottle holder
	Disposable liners (need to be replaced)
	Nipples which need to be cleaned (automatic dishwashing is generally considered sufficient)
Reusable bottles	Comfortable number is 8 bottles
	Nipples/caps
	Cleaning considerations (automatic dishwashers are generally acceptable; electric and stovetop sterilizers are available)
Bottle holder in the refrigerator	Use a six- or eight-pack soda holder to keep bottles upright and organized in the refrigerator

Bottle Feeding Routine

• Are all supplies (bottles, nipples) clean?

• Is formula fresh? Get into the habit of marking directly on the can the day and time that the formula was opened or mixed. Do not keep formula in a can for more than 24 hours.

• Is baby getting formula through the nipple?

• Is baby semi-upright? The baby should not lie flat while feeding; this increases the chances for ear infections.

• Did you change sides while feeding the baby? This helps eye coordination.

• Do you have a burp cloth handy? Formula stains clothing—both yours and baby's.

• Is baby showing any signs of constipation which you need to report to the doctor?

Breastfeeding Considerations

Nursing preparations

- Go braless. The friction created between the nipple and the cloth of your blouse will toughen the skin.
- Expose your nipples to air.
- Rub nipples daily with a towel after your bath or shower to toughen them and prepare them for nursing.
- Ask your childbirth instructor if the hospital has a good breastfeeding coach who helps you get started.
- Consider purchasing the following supplies:

    Nursing bras: Be professionally fitted at a maternity shop and purchase the bras toward the end of the pregnancy.

    Nursing pads: Disposable nursing pads are available. Less expensive alternatives include cut-up diapers and cut-up sanitary pads. Washable pads are also available at most maternity shops. Less expensive alternatives include men's handkerchiefs, cut-up toweling and dishcloths.

    Waterproof pads: Protect your mattress against stains created by leakage at night.

- Supplies for expressing milk:

    Pump (electric or hand)

    Bottles, nipples (Disposable bottle liners are more convenient for freezing milk).

Clothing considerations

- Front-buttoning blouses/dresses/robes (Pay special attention to color. A busy pattern will hide leakage but will make you look larger.)
- Husband's old button-front shirts
- Smock-styled blouses and dresses (be sure the top of the garment lowers sufficiently for nursing or that the smock has tie straps)
- Oversized blouse styles, particularly those which are loose at the waist. You can nurse more discreetly by lifting your blouse instead of unbuttoning it.
- Nursing gowns (available at maternity clothing shops or maternity departments within retail stores)
- Nursing slips or half slips

Pediatricians

Around the sixth month of your pregnancy you will be encouraged to select a pediatrician. You will spend a great deal of time at the doctor's office for well-baby visits during the first year. Many a pediatrician has jokingly accused patients of owning corporate stock in their practice. The important thing is that you like, trust and are comfortable with your pediatrician.

Understanding the Terminology

Physician	Graduate of a certified medical school. May or may not be affiliated with a hospital.
Board-certified	Physician who has selected a specialty and has passed the requirements of the American Board of Specialties. Generally, these requirements include three years of additional training in a hospital and an examination. The specialty can be in any one of numerous fields or in a combination of fields.
FAAP	Fellow of the American Academy of Pediatrics. Board-certified and a member of this pediatric honorary society. Generally accepted as having very complete pediatric training.

Resources for Finding Your Baby's Physician

- The hospital nursery nursing staff. (This is a similar situation to selecting an obstetrical caregiver. Nurses see the physicians at work with both mothers and babies and, therefore, can give you excellent advice and information.

- Friends with children. (Ask them the same questions you intend to ask during the pediatrician's interview.)

- Family physician or family practitioner (if you intend to have a pediatrician as opposed to a family practice physician).

- American Medical Association local chapter

- Mothers in childbirth classes

- Health maintenance organization

- Teaching hospitals

Pediatrician Evaluator

It is important to interview your child's caregiver. Because many physicians only accept newborns into their practice, it can be very difficult to change if you are unhappy with the medical care you receive. There may be a charge for this appointment, but it is money well spent. Some physicians credit your account for the fee of the interview if you choose their practice. Below are several questions and observations to keep in mind.

Name: _____ Telephone Number: _____

Appointment Date: _____

Educational training and professional development

With which hospitals are you affiliated? _____

Are you board-certified? _____ What specialty? _____

Length of time in practice? _____

Are you involved with a teaching hospital? _____
(Teaching hospitals are associated with medical schools. Many physicians who are associated with these hospitals are involved in the training of other doctors, and, therefore, remain current on medical developments.)

Accessibility

What hours and days is the office open? _____

When are you at the office? _____

Can you accommodate working mothers? _____

What are the provisions for emergencies when the office is closed? _____

How are routine questions answered? _____

Do you have a phone-in session when I can speak directly to you? _____

What are the hours? _____

What is your weekend schedule? _____

Are you in a group? _____

If so, can I meet the other group members? _____

Can I call you at home? _____

Medical style

How supportive are you toward breast-feeding? _____

How supportive are you toward bottle feeding? _____

Do you give information on developmental stages of the child? _____

Will I be given the weight and height of my child for entry
into a growth chart? _____

Do you explain the weight and height of my child? (Many physicians compare the information to a national norm.) _____

Do you give out sample medication so that I can try the medication before filling the prescription? _____

Support personnel

What are the roles of the nurse and receptionist? _____

Does the nurse answer medical questions? _____
Are you aware of mother and baby activities within the community? _____
Do you make recommendations on classes, baby literature or other child-related activities? _____

Office

Are well-baby and sick-baby appointments kept separated? _____
What is the average time spent waiting? _____
Does the office handle insurance forms? _____
  (Once you learn how to complete the insurance forms it might be to your advantage to do your own paperwork. When you eventually learn what the policy covers, you can combine doctor's visits—i.e. exam for cradle cap, which generally is covered, with a well-baby visit, which generally is not covered. In that way, a portion of the well-baby visit fee is defrayed.)
Do you accept checks? _____ Major credit cards? _____
Will the office bill me for an appointment? _____
  (It can be difficult writing a check with a baby in tow.)
Will I be billed for appointments when I am late? _____
Will I be billed for no-show appointments? _____
Does your office call to remind me of scheduled appointments? _____
How are routine appointments scheduled? _____

Other considerations

Did the physician ask you questions? _____
  • Your family health history _____
  • Your schedule after the baby arrives _____
  • Your intentions to breast or bottle feed _____
  • Your fears and anxieties _____
How accessible is the office to your home, office or babysitter? _____
Was the office pleasant? _____ Clean? _____
Toys and books for the children? _____
Did you and your husband feel comfortable? _____

Baby Medical Care Organizer

Use the following checklist to organize your observations of your baby. The information will be useful to your pediatrician at well-baby visits and will assist you in remembering all the things you want to discuss with the doctor. By being prepared, you can provide more accurate information.

Doctor's name _____ Telephone (Office) _____

(Home) _____

Pharmacy name _____ Telephone _____

Symptom	Comments	Yes	No
Feeding			
Duration/amount	_____ minutes for breastfed babies or		
	_____ounces for bottle-fed babies		
Frequency	_____minutes every _____hours		
Supplemental feedings	Name of supplement: _____ amount _____		
Satisfaction	Does the baby appear to be satisfied?	☐	☐
Vomiting	Does the baby vomit or spit up?	☐	☐
	Is vomiting projectile?	☐	☐
	Quantity of spit-up or vomit as a percentage of intake: _____		
	Frequency of vomiting:		
	Every feeding?	☐	☐
	Every _____ minutes/hours		
Elimination			
Soiled diapers	Frequency of wet diaper: every _____ minute/hours		
	Frequency of bowel movement: every _____ minute/hours		
Appearance of bowel movement	Is it tinged with blood?	☐	☐
	Is it watery?	☐	☐
	Color change from _____ to _____		
	Texture change from _____ to _____		
Baby's reaction	Baby's reaction during elimination:		
	• Cries	☐	☐
	• Forced reaction (baby red in the face)	☐	☐
	• Grimacing	☐	☐
Fever			
Temperature	_____ F. rectal? or axillary?		
	_____ C. rectal? or axillary?		
	Duration of temperature: _____		

Methods used to reduce temperature	• Dress in lightweight clothing • Dress in diaper only • Sponge with lukewarm water • Soak in lukewarm tub
Fluid intake	Type(s) of fluid _____ Quantity/frequency: _____ minutes of nursing _____ounces of bottle

Skin appearance

Is there one of the following rashes:
- Blotched ☐ ☐
- Solid color ☐ ☐
- Crustated with pus or blood ☐ ☐
- Cheesy ☐ ☐

Is baby's coloring one of the following:
- Flushed ☐ ☐
- Pale ☐ ☐
- Yellow (jaundiced) ☐ ☐

Crying

Duration _____
Is there any pattern? ☐ ☐
(time of day, location) _____
_____

Do comforting techniques soothe the baby?

Sleeping activity

Sleeps _____ hours per day
Sleeps _____ hours per night
Alert while awake? ☐ ☐
Fitful sleeper? ☐ ☐
Convulsive? ☐ ☐

Other activities

Pulling at ears ☐ ☐
Rubbing eyes ☐ ☐
Pulling legs into a prenatal tuck ☐ ☐
Jerky movements ☐ ☐
Convulsive ☐ ☐

Doctor's instructions: _____
_____
_____

Medication

Name: _____

Dosage: _____

Frequency: _____

Attention

Watch for: _____

_____

Duration

Make appointment if not improved by: _____

Baby's Immunization Checklist

Immunization schedule recommended by the American Academy of Pediatrics:

Given	Age	Immunization	Date Given	Given By
☐	2 months	DPT* Trivalent oral polio	_____	_____
☐	4 months	DPT Trivalent oral polio	_____	_____
☐	6 months	DPT	_____	_____
☐	1 year	Tuberculine test	_____	_____
☐	15 months	Measles, mumps, rubella	_____	_____
☐	18 months	DPT Trivalent oral polio	_____	_____
☐	4-6 years	DPT Trivalent oral polio	_____	_____

*Diphtheria, Pertussis and Tetanus

Chapter Three
Mother's Needs

Maternity Clothing and Other Essentials

You're dressing for two now, but it doesn't necessarily mean a whole new wardrobe. Friends and relatives are usually glad to help out and maternity clothes are easy to sew.

Practical Maternity Clothing Checklist

Item	Features
Sweatsuits	Comfortable for early pregnancy and postpartum.
	Bright colors stimulate baby.
	Soft cotton is soothing for newborn and mom.
Bib overalls	Waistless style is good for postpartum and early pregnancy.
	Prepregnancy blouses (only top buttons closed) can be worn beneath bibs, adding variety to your wardrobe. You can also say that you are in your prepregnancy clothes!
	Pockets are very handy for baby items.
Wrap-around skirts	Comfortable if you have difficult episiotomy.
	Adjustable waist is good for postpartum and early pregnancy.
Elastic waistbands	Comfortable in early pregnancy and postpartum.
Husband's front-button shirts	Cover-ups to protect shoulders of mother's clothes from baby's spit-up stains.
	Good for nursing.
Middle-weight fabric	Your pregnancy and postpartum will span several seasons. Extend your clothing by adding sweaters or sleeveless blouses.
Homemade clothes	Sewing allows you to individualize your clothing at a lower cost. Protect your maternity clothing against stains with Scotchguard.

Borrowed Maternity Clothing Organizer

Another real money saver is borrowing maternity clothes from friends. If you borrow maternity clothes, use the following chart to keep track of the outfits. There is a space to mark the condition of the clothing. In many cases, maternity outfits are coming to you directly from another borrower. The owner may be unaware of the poor condition of her maternity wear. Take a moment to document problems such as stains, rips, missing buttons, broken zippers and worn elastic. The list protects you against possible hurt feelings later.

Owner	Article Code*	Color	Condition

* Code as follows:

D = Dress	NG = Nursing Gown	H = Shorts
S = Slacks	MS = Maternity Slip	SW = Swimming
P = Pantyhose	B = Blouse	NB = Nursing Bra

Return the clothing toward the end of your pregnancy. After the baby arrives, you'll be too preoccupied. Clean and repair any damage done. Remember the loaner with a small gift either for herself or her child.

Mother's Wish List

Consider making your life much easier by purchasing or borrowing the following survival equipment.

Want	Have	Item	Advantages
☐	☐	Hand-held shower nozzle	Useful for the episiotomy. Useful for washing child's hair.
☐	☐	Hand-held heat lamp	Useful for the episiotomy.
☐	☐	Cordless telephone	Allows you to accept long-distance congratulatory calls without getting out of bed. Allows you to continue nursing, changing or rocking the baby while talking on the phone.

☐	☐	Answering machine	Useful for sending out information and announcements. Also handy when you are unable to make it to the phone.
☐	☐	Hand-held radio/cassette player with headphones	Listen to music instead of a colicky baby. Also provides you with sing-along music for the baby.
☐	☐	Clock radio with timer	The music can be settling to the baby. The timer can also gently awaken a baby that sleeps through a feeding.
☐	☐	Large overstuffed reading pillow with side arms	Helpful for leverage and back support if you intend to nurse upright in bed. Can be put into the corner of the playpen when baby is learning to sit.
☐	☐	Water pillow	Partially filled water pillows under mommy's tummy can help support the weight. Also, gently rocking a newborn on a waterbed/pillow can have a soothing effect.
☐	☐	Penlight or flashlight	Great for checking on baby in a dark room. Always leave it in a handy spot.
☐	☐	Dimmer switch	Place a dimmer switch (or ask a qualified friend to do it as a gift) in the nursery's overhead light. Dim light is less disruptive at 2 a.m. than full light.
☐	☐	Programmable digital watch	Very helpful for nursing moms. You can keep track of the duration of nursing and the time since the last nursing began.
☐	☐	Tape recorder	Record your thoughts and those of your friends when they come to visit. Later, use it to tape your child's vocabulary development.
☐	☐	Hair blower	Set on low cool; a blower helps both an episiotomy and the baby's diaper rash.
☐	☐	Intercom	Battery-powered models allow you to carry the intercom receiver out of the house. Electrical variety requires an outlet and is confined to the house.

Mother's Medication and Hygiene Organizer

Consult with your caregiver during prenatal checkups regarding the items below. Consider stocking up on these items and having them at home when you return from the hospital.

Need	Have	Item	Comments
☐	☐	Over-the-counter analgesics: aspirin and acetaminophen	Consult your doctor, especially if you are breastfeeding.
☐	☐	Analgesic sprays	For perineal care: Consult a physician for recommendations.
☐	☐	Sitz bath	Many hospitals provide you with a take-home sitz bath. If your hospital does, borrow a sitz bath from a friend prior to delivery and learn how to use it in your bathroom. Many sitz baths work on gravity flow (the waterbag must be higher than the seat). This can be accomplished by putting the bag on a door hook or by hooking the bag onto the toilet tank with a hanger.
☐	☐	Premoistened pads	The pads feel more comfortable if kept cool; keep them in the refrigerator or in an ice bucket.
☐	☐	Foam ring	Used as a sitting aid.
☐	☐	Hemorrhoid cream	Ask for your physician's recommendation.
☐	☐	Enema	Have one on hand in the event that diet does not correct constipation difficulties.
☐	☐	Breast cream	For sore or cracked nipples.
☐	☐	Nursing pads	
☐	☐	Panty liners	
☐	☐	Sanitary pads	

Special Treats for the "Lady in Waiting"

In addition to all of the activities in this workbook, consider doing some of the following during the last days of your pregnancy:

"Take Care of Mommy" List

- Get hair done. Make an appointment for your due date so that the day will not be a total loss if the baby is past due.
- Manicure
- Pedicure
- Facial
- Makeup makeover
- Dinner out with your spouse or a close friend
- Plan religious ceremony (see chapter 8)
- Have a baby shower
- Go shopping
- Work on handicrafts for the baby
- Have friends in for a visit (Invite other mothers from childbirth classes with or without babies, but no labor tales!)
- Take in a movie/theater (aisle seats toward the back)
- Stage your own film festival with rented videos on your VCR. (If you don't own a VCR, now is the time to rent one so you can watch movies in the comfort of your own home.)
- Visit the local art museum or gallery; it may be awhile before you get another opportunity.
- Drop by the library to stock up on your favorite reading material for those first few weeks after baby comes home.
- If you have a tape player, borrow taped novels and non-fiction from the library. Even if you don't have the time to sit and read, you can always pop in a cassette for listening to as you take care of your new baby.

38

Reading List

Pregnancy is nine months long, so you have enough time to read about what to expect. Keep track of the books you have read, books you would like to read, books you own and books you would like to buy for yourself. See the Appendix for a list of baby books.

Library Organizer

Author/Title	Want to Read	Have Read	Own	Would Like as Gift	Borrowed From
	☐	☐	☐	☐	
	☐	☐	☐	☐	
	☐	☐	☐	☐	
	☐	☐	☐	☐	
	☐	☐	☐	☐	
	☐	☐	☐	☐	
	☐	☐	☐	☐	
	☐	☐	☐	☐	
	☐	☐	☐	☐	
	☐	☐	☐	☐	
	☐	☐	☐	☐	
	☐	☐	☐	☐	

Chapter Four
Baby's Needs

Choosing a Name

One of the most important things your baby will need is a name. Consider the following checklist of ideas when naming your child.

Naming Checklist

• Namesake	Is it livable for a child? An adult? Do you perceive any problems with Jr., III, etc.?
• Religion	Does your religion have naming guidelines? Some Catholics prefer saints' names. Some Jews prefer to not use names of living relatives and often opt for biblical names. Some Muslims prefer Islamic names.
• Gender	Do you want a unisex name (i.e. Lee)?
• Number of names	Remember most forms provide for a first, middle and last name.
• Sounds	Avoid puns and rhythmical names, as well as awkward sounds.
• Rhythms	Generally, unequal numbers of syllables in the first, middle and last names create a good rhythmic sound.
• Pronunciation	Will the name be pronounceable (on the basis of the spelling) to a stranger?
• Spelling	Consider the consequences of "creative" spelling vs. traditional spelling of a name.
• Popularity	What are your feelings about giving your child a name which six other children in his or her class will have? Or what will your child encounter if you select a very unpopular or odd-sounding name which no one else in school has (or wants)?
• Uniqueness	Consider balancing the child's first and middle names with a mixture of a common name with a unique name (especially if the surname is either very unique or very common).

- Stereotypes — Check for both good and bad associations with a particular name.

- Initials — Avoid combining names which result in a monogram that spells out a funny word such as BUG or RAT. If you use your intitials, you can pass monogrammed heirlooms down more easily.

- Nicknames — Consider the nicknames associated with your child's name. Beware of giving your child a nickname as a legal name as they may spend a lifetime explaining their name.

- Meanings — Know the meanings of your child's name (particularly if you're superstitious).

Baby's Clothes

Obtain a layette list from your local store or use the one provided below. Weigh the expense of duplicating newborn clothes against the need for frequent laundering.

Use the following worksheet to keep track of the items in the layette which you have already purchased or borrowed. A current inventory can save you money and time and prevent the purchase of duplicate items. Save your receipts so you can return any purchases if you receive similar items as gifts.

Layette List

Item	Estimated Number Required	Number On Hand	Number Borrowed	Borrowed From
Cloth diapers	4 dozen or 1-2 dozen, if using diaper service or disposables	_____	_____	_____
Disposable diapers	350 the first month	_____	_____	_____
Waterproof pants (for cloth diapers)	4-6	_____	_____	_____
Undershirts:				
Newborn	optional	_____	_____	_____
Small	6	_____	_____	_____

Gowns or kimonos	4-6	_____	_____	_____
Stretch suits	3-4	_____	_____	_____
Sweaters	1	_____	_____	_____
Blanket sleeper	1-2	_____	_____	_____
Bibs	2-4	_____	_____	_____
Safety diaper pins (double-locking heads; needed only for cloth diapers)	4	_____	_____	_____
Bunting (winter baby)	1	_____	_____	_____
Sunsuit/diaper sets	optional	_____	_____	_____
Socks	optional	_____	_____	_____
Booties	4-6	_____	_____	_____
Crib sheets	4-6	_____	_____	_____
Crib blankets	2-3	_____	_____	_____
Receiving blankets	3-5	_____	_____	_____
Waterproof lap pads	2-6	_____	_____	_____
Flannelette coated sheets	2	_____	_____	_____
Quilted crib pads	2	_____	_____	_____
Wash cloths	6	_____	_____	_____
Hand towels	2-3	_____	_____	_____
Hooded bath towels	2-3	_____	_____	_____
Infant seat cover		_____	_____	_____
Playpen cover		_____	_____	_____
Car seat cover		_____	_____	_____
High chair cover		_____	_____	_____
Diaper bag		_____	_____	_____
Other:				
_____		_____	_____	_____
_____		_____	_____	_____
_____		_____	_____	_____
_____		_____	_____	_____
_____		_____	_____	_____
_____		_____	_____	_____
_____		_____	_____	_____

Baby Clothing Sizing Chart

Size is determined by height and weight, not age.

Size	Height	Weight
Newborn	to 24 inches	to 14 pounds
Small	24½ to 28 inches	15 to 20 pounds
Medium	28½ to 32 inches	21 to 26 pounds
Large	23½ to 36 inches	27 to 32 pounds
X-large	36½ to 38 inches	33 to 36 pounds

Infant sleepwear runs slightly smaller than the above sizes:

Size	Height	Weight
Newborn	to 23 inches	to 13 pounds
1B	23½ to 26 inches	14 to 17 pounds
2B	26½ to 29 inches	18 to 22 pounds
3B	29½ to 32 inches	23 to 26 pounds
4B	32½ to 35 inches	27 to 31 pounds

Newborn Clothing Evaluator

Evaluate your newborn's clothing on the basis of changeability, safety, washability, growing room and neutrality (if you intend to have another child).

Yes	No	Changeability

Consideration

Yes	No	
☐	☐	Front snap shirts (easier than pullovers)?
☐	☐	Crotch snaps on both legs (easier to diaper)?
☐	☐	One-piece (the more pieces, the longer it takes to change)?
☐	☐	Ties/buttons/snaps in front?
☐	☐	Full cut (especially if you double diaper the baby)?
☐	☐	Drawstrings or encased elastic?

Safety

Yes	No	
☐	☐	Flame retardant fabric?
☐	☐	Are bows and buttons securely fastened?
☐	☐	No loose threads that could entangle baby's fingers or toes and cut off circulation?
☐	☐	Is the garment large enough around neck, arms and legs?
☐	☐	Manufacturer clearly identified?
☐	☐	Will baby be protected against irritation from zippers, etc.?

Washability

☐ ☐ Colorfast fabric including trim and appliques?
☐ ☐ Permanent press finish?
☐ ☐ Machine washable and dryable?
☐ ☐ Detachable coordinated bibs?
☐ ☐ Sturdy seams which will not unravel?
☐ ☐ Comfortable fabric (soft on baby's skin)?

Growing room

☐ ☐ Full cut?
☐ ☐ Adequate length in arms and legs?
☐ ☐ If outfit has more than one piece, will any pieces still be wearable after baby has outgrown a portion of the outfit (i.e. vests are generally wearable after pants have been outgrown)?
☐ ☐ Adjustable snaps to allow for growth?

Neutrality

☐ ☐ Can this outfit be worn by another child of the opposite sex?

Economizing Strategies

Three basic problems generally are associated with dressing children: outgrown clothes; stained clothing; and, clothing which "falls apart." Strategies on how to deal with these situations are as follows:

Size

- Purchase small instead of newborn sizes, especially if there is a family history of large babies. If clothes are too big, swaddle baby in blankets and stuff cotton balls in the feet of booties or one-piece stretch suits.
- Multiple-pieced outfits provide more flexibility. Larger-sized portions of the original outfit can still be worn when smaller pieces do not fit.
- Buy clothes that allow for simple adjustments as baby grows larger; clothing that can be released by snaps, straps and buckles.
- Cut the foot hem out of stretch suits and place baby into booties.
- Purchase clothing made of fabrics which "give" such as terry cloth or knits.

Stains (Or: Wouldn't it be wonderful to have a laundress?)

Don't despair, there are cheaper alternatives than replacement. But before attacking an infant stain, remember two things: First, follow the manufacturer's instructions on the label. Second, weigh the potential risks of chemical exposure to your newborn against a spotless white laundry. Some stains are basic to newborns: formula, spit-up, baby oil, elimination and vitamins. Do not allow any of these stains to "set" by putting them into the hamper or by washing untreated clothing in hot water. Prompt action is important.

* Select clothing designs which hide the common stains of infancy:

  outfits with bright splashes of color

  outfits with appliques and detachable bibs

* Consider hot vs. cold water wash:

  Cool wash water minimizes fabric wear, permanently setting stains, running colors and energy costs.

  Hot water helps destroy bacteria and is, therefore, suited to diapers and underwear of natural fibers.

* Consider natural vs. synthetic fabrics:

  Natural fabrics are generally softer, more absorbent, "breathe" better than synthetic fabrics and tolerate hot and sterilizing temperatures.

  Natural fabrics are less resistant to mildew, fungus, insect damage and shrinkage than synthetics.

  Synthetic fabrics are "easy care" if washed in lukewarm water and removed promptly from a warm dryer.

  Synthetic fabrics keep body temperatures higher in summer and cooler in winter because the fabrics do not "breathe."

Removing elimination

You'll find this on cloth diapers or on other baby clothes due to leakage of disposable diapers. To remove the soil, perform the following steps:

1. Swish the soiled diaper in the toilet to remove any bowel movement. (Diaper liners allow you to bypass this task. Disposable diaper liners are inexpensive and also work as a wick, drawing urine moisture away from the baby's skin.)

2. Allow diapers or soiled clothing to soak in a pail containing one of the following: enzyme presoak (non-chlorine bleach), Dreft, Lysol, Pine Sol, Borax.

3. Machine wash in hot water.

4. Rinse twice. (Do not use large amounts of fabric softener; it decreases the diapers' ability to absorb).

5. Dry plastic pants on the no-heat fluff cycle of your dryer.

Post the following chart in your laundry room.

Infant Stain Chart

Stain	Pre-washing Instructions	De-Spot Chemical	Washing Instructions
Petroleum jelly	Scrape off Use an absorbent	Oil-base solvent	Wash in washing machine; repeat until clean
Ointment	Blot or use an absorbent	Oil-base solvent	Wash in washing machine; repeat until clean.
Medicine with high sugar such as vitamins or tempra		1-oil base 2-alcohol 3-combination solvent	Wash in washing machine; if 1st washing doesn't work try 2nd and 3rd combination
Spit-up	Flush with water immediately	Diluted ammonia	Wash in washing machine; repeat until clean.
Urine	Flush with water	1) Ammonia followed by vinegar or lemon or 2) Enzyme paste for 20 minutes	Wash in washing machine; if 1st is unsuccessful, try 2nd combination
Blood	Blot then rinse with cool water	1) Enzyme paste 2) Ammonia	Wash in washing machine; if 1st is unsuccessful, try 2nd combination

Quality

The third cause of unnecessary clothing expense is poor quality and construction. As a consumer, you are entitled to quality workmanship. If the clothing (or any other baby item) does not withstand normal use, write the manufacturer. Many companies welcome your comments in order to improve their product. Generally, they will replace the item. If they do not offer to replace the item, suggest that they do so in your return letter. Here are some hints on settling a claim.

1. If you still have the receipt, return it to the store where it was purchased and let them deal with the manufacturer.

2. Obtain the accurate address of the company. This information is listed in *Standard and Poor's* and is available over the phone by calling your public library (business division). Address the letter to the company's consumer complaint division, quality control or general office.

3. Be specific in your complaint. List the difficulties you have encountered (i.e. elastic which has pulled away from the stitching, notions that have fallen off, snaps that have pulled loose, flaws in the fabric, colorfast problems or poor seam construction).

4. Indicate the amount of wear or use the article has received. This is especially true if only one child has worn the outfit rarely.

5. Include your full name, address, date and telephone number on the return address. Always list the date for easier reference in the event the company does not respond to your initial letter. Include your telephone number. A company employee may contact you by phone to discuss the problems rather than write.

6. Make copies of all correspondence. Note the date the letter was mailed on the copy.

7. Send another letter if the first one is unsuccessful. Be slightly more indignant in the second letter, being angry about the quality and also about their attitude. Send copies to the president of the company and, if the product is unsafe, to the Consumer Product Safety Commission (1750 K St. N.W., Washington D.C. 20207). Indicate on the letter that copies are being sent to the commission.

Sample letter

226 W. Elm St.
Westwood, PA 00000
September 1, 1986
(412) 555-8675 home
(412) 555-7352 office

Consumer Division/Quality Control
Easy Care Clothes
333 N. Main St.
Willow, AL 00000

Dear Sir:
  I purchased an Easy Care Clothes outfit in August for my daughter. It was a three-month-size stretch suit. After four washings, the applique has faded, the elastic at the right foot has become unstitched and two buttons fell off easily.
  I am very disappointed with this stretch suit. Certainly this is not indicative of your company's standard of quality? I hope to hear from you soon regarding this problem.
                                        Sincerely,

If no response is received from the initial correspondence, send a follow-up letter.

Sample follow-up letter

226 W. Elm St.
Westwood, PA 00000
October 1, 1986
(412) 555-8675 home
(412) 555-7352 office

Consumer Division/Quality Control
Easy Care Clothes
333 N. Main St.
Willow, AL 00000

Dear Sir:
  On September 1, 1986, I wrote you regarding a problem concerning an article of clothing manufactured by Easy Care Clothes. See the attached copy of the letter. As of today's date, there has been no response. Am I to assume that the lack of correspondence is an affirmation of Easy Care Clothes' poor quality and workmanship?
  My initial concern was the limited use my daughter received from the garment. Upon further thought, I am now concerned with the safety of the suit. It would be very easy for a child to pull off one of the poorly attached buttons and choke on it. Perhaps the Consumer Product Safety Commission should investigate this matter.
  I look forward to your response.
                                        Sincerely,

cc: John Doe, President, Easy Care Clothing
    Consumer Product Safety Commission

Baby Clothing Organizer

One of the most popular ways to stretch a clothing budget is to share with friends. The following system can be used for loaned clothing when the owner eventually wants her baby clothes returned. It is very easy to be overwhelmed with boxes and bags of unmarked and unsorted clothing.

1. Purchase permanent marking pens in a variety of colors. Sets of pens are available in craft stores.

2. Assign each friend who has loaned you clothes both an individual initial (usually the last name) and an individual color.

3. Mark all clothing by initial and color. The double coding ensures against faded markings after frequent washing.

4. Sort all clothing by size, disregarding ownership.

5. Place clothing into boxes, layering the larger sizes at the bottom and the smaller sizes toward the top.

6. As your child outgrows the clothing, place all outfits (disregarding ownership) into a storage box.

7. Periodically sort the outgrown clothes box by ownership and return.

Baby Clothing Storage

Organizing your baby clothes is helpful if you have a second child or if you loan baby clothing to friends. Follow the simple suggestions below:

1. Mark baby clothing with your initial only after the baby has actually worn the outfit. You might be able to return or exchange unused baby outfits if unmarked. Unused, unmarked clothing also can be used as a gift.

2. Make labels and attach to storage boxes. Empty disposable diaper boxes of the appropriate size and empty toy boxes are convenient. (If space is available, keep manufacturers' boxes. That way you have an address to write to if the article is inferior or you need replacement parts. Also, if you choose to have a garage sale, items with their original boxes get higher prices.)

3. Number the boxes to provide you with a growth sequence. It will be easier to find the appropriate size if you know the baby has outgrown Box 6 rather than an age or weight.

Baby's Medicine Cabinet Checklist

To Buy	On Hand	Item
		Toiletries
☐	☐	Disposable diapers (purchase in both newborn and small sizes)
☐	☐	Diaper liners (good for cloth and inexpensive disposable diapers)
☐	☐	Masking tape (use to refasten diapers when tabs no longer work)
☐	☐	Baby oil
☐	☐	Petroleum jelly
☐	☐	Baby wipes
☐	☐	Baby soap (check with pediatrician)
☐	☐	Baby lotion
☐	☐	Baby powder
☐	☐	Baby shampoo
☐	☐	Sterile cotton balls
☐	☐	Hangers for clothing

Medical supplies (Use only under physician's direction)

To Buy	On Hand	Item
☐	☐	Diaper rash cream or ointment
☐	☐	Petroleum jelly
☐	☐	Infant acetaminophen
☐	☐	Digital thermometer (The quick readable display is very reassuring for novices.)
☐	☐	Pacifier with temperature dot (If your baby has a fever the temperature dot on the pacifier will darken.)
☐	☐	Alcohol for the umbilical cord
☐	☐	Syringe with markings for liquid medication drops (These handy medication dispensers come with an insert to place into the medicine bottle, enabling you to extract the medication more easily.)
☐	☐	Sun shield (check with pediatrician)
☐	☐	Nasal aspirator
☐	☐	Cool mist vaporizer
☐	☐	Blunt edge nail scissors (Invest in a good manicure scissors. It can always be used for sewing later.)

Equipping the Nursery

What follows is a list of the many items available for the nursery, along with suggestions for cheaper alternatives and multiple uses of items.

Nursery and Equipment Checklist

Item	To Buy	On Hand	Alternative
Bassinet	☐	☐	Laundry basket
	☐	☐	Dresser drawer set on a flat surface
	☐	☐	Perambulator or baby buggy
Cradle	☐	☐	Baby swing with both a bed and seat attachment
Moses basket	☐	☐	Laundry basket with handles
	☐	☐	Infant carrier (also known as a "pumpkin seat")
	☐	☐	Portable infant car seat carrier
Crib	☐	☐	
Crib mattress			
Crib bumper	☐	☐	Bumper pads are very easy to make and many patterns are available at fabric stores. Or you can slipcover a less expensive bumper.
			Note: The bumper should be attached to the crib in a minimum of six locations. Attach with ribbons or twill tape.
Intrauterine sounds	☐	☐	These are often tape recordings placed inside a stuffed animal. Special sound effects albums or tapes are available at most public libraries. (Not all babies are comforted by intrauterine or special sound effects.)
Portable crib	☐	☐	Collapsible playpen
	☐	☐	Well-padded dresser drawer
	☐	☐	Perambulator or reclining stroller
Baby bath	☐	☐	Use a sink or any large plastic container and line with towels or foam padding. If you request an egg shell foam mattress at the hospital, bring it home for the baby's foam-padded bath.
Baby swing with chair and bed	☐	☐	See "Cradle."

Dresser	☐	☐	
Changing table	☐	☐	
Diaper pail	☐	☐	Diaper services usually provide one. Use step-on trash cans with lids and plastic liners for either cloth or disposable diapers. The lids help control odors, the liners aid in cleanup, and the step-on feature is safe and efficient.
Diaper bag	☐	☐	Any large carrier can be divided into easily organized sections. An accordian file, available at office supply stores, is a great divider.
Laundry hamper	☐	☐	
Extra bed for caregiver	☐	☐	Flip-flop chair which opens into a bed and can be used later as a chair.
Car seat (Be sure the seat you select meets current federal safety standards.)			
Mobiles (Consider using mobiles in areas other than the crib, such as the changing table, stroller and infant seat.)	☐	☐	Mobiles are very simple to make, inexpensive and more flexible than commercial ones. Safely secure brightly colored objects onto yarn or a hanger. String the yarn across the rails of the crib or suspend the hanger from a hook on the wall or ceiling. Anchor the mobile with the baby's vantage point in mind: A newborn's range of vision is approximately eight inches, so do not mount it too high, and remember that these objects are to be seen from below, not from the side. (See safety evaluator on page 54.)
Stroller	☐	☐	
Playpen	☐	☐	A child's hard plastic swimming pool can be substituted for a newborn's playpen, but is not as mobile.
Lamp	☐	☐	Install a dimmer switch for more flexibility in lighting.
Walker (Walkers with locking wheels can also be used as the first feeding chair.)	☐	☐	
Jumper or exerciser	☐	☐	
Rocking chair	☐	☐	

Decorating the Nursery

- Use nursery wallpaper border instead of nursery wallpaper.
- Cut large, bold, geometric shapes from contact paper. Place these shapes on the wall, furniture and ceilings.
- Decorate with functional items. If you receive several adorable crib blankets, hang them on the wall on curtain rods or tacked directly onto the wall.
- Decorate with plants and planters you receive. Keep the decorative pots and use them to store such items as cotton balls, scented candles, safety pins, hair brushes and toiletries.
- Consider using less orthodox furniture in the nursery. Items such as metal storage shelves and plastic crates give a high-tech look and also provide you with more storage. Be sure to anchor them securely to the wall.
- Allow baby's gifts of stuffed animals to be the room's focal point. Place the animals on shelves, or put them in windows or on curtain rods, or suspend them on ribbons from the ceiling or hooks on the wall.
- Avoid decorating in pink or blue until the baby is born. Don't count on your instincts—it can be an expensive mistake. The following neutral themes are good for both boys and girls: teddy bears, clowns, ducks, rabbits, cartoon characters, fairy tale figures, letters of the alphabet, numbers, kites, balloons, clouds, or rainbows.

Keeping Baby's Development in Mind

- Use mirrors in the nursery. Locate mirrors strategically (such as on the wall opposite the crib or rocking chair) to see the baby while he is being held on your shoulder or resting in the crib.
- Place something interesting behind the rocking chair and the changing table to give baby something to focus upon, such as a mobile, wind chime (to stimulate the baby through sound), wall hanging, mirror, or picture.
- Use brightly patterned sheets. Infants respond favorably to bright colors.
- Place sun catchers or crystal prisms in the window.

Purchasing Baby Equipment

If you are purchasing new nursery equipment, approach a store with several members of your childbirth class and ask the store if they give volume discounts. Many stores give coupon discounts to various hospitals and clinics. Inform the store salesperson that you intend to deliver at one of the participating hospitals and ask for a discount. Much of the recently designed youth furniture and equipment has multiple uses, resulting in obvious savings. Such examples include:

- A crib which converts to a juvenile bed
- A changing table which converts to a dresser
- A high chair which converts to a juvenile booster chair
- A perambulator which converts to a stroller

Improving Older Baby Equipment

• Repaint in high-gloss nontoxic paint.

• Decorate furniture with large decals to coordinate with those on the nursery walls. Selection includes cartoon characters, animals and fairy tales; they are available in baby stores or through advertisements in baby magazines.

• Use remaining wallpaper or wallpaper scraps to cut out letters, animals or number forms and glue on the exterior crib headboard or dresser; frame or border the crib or dresser; or cover changing table shelves, bookcase shelves or line drawers.

• Purchase or make covers for worn furniture. The following covers are commercially available: high chairs, plastic infant carriers, car seats and play yards. King-size pillowcases fit standard size changing table pads.

Nursery Safety Checklist

Yes	No	Consideration
☐	☐	Has assembly of the equipment been checked? (Hint: Place a ten-pound potato bag where baby will lie. It is much safer than testing by hand.)
☐	☐	Is equipment free of potentially dangerous carvings or designs?
☐	☐	Has the equipment or furniture been checked for loose nuts, bolts, screws, nails and handles? (This is especially important for equipment which swings or has movable parts.)
☐	☐	Is the equipment free of splinters, blistered paint, and loose pieces?
☐	☐	Are all painted surfaces non-lead based and nontoxic?
☐	☐	Does the bumper tie to the crib rails in at least six locations?
☐	☐	Is the distance between the crib slats 2⅜ inches or less?
☐	☐	Does the mattress fit tightly within the crib?
☐	☐	Is the top of the lowered crib side at least 9 inches above mattress at its highest position and, when raised, at least 26 inches above the mattress at its lowest position?
☐	☐	Are teething rails safely secured and atop each crib side?
☐	☐	Is there sufficient clearance from the wall for equipment which swings, such as cradles and baby swings?
☐	☐	Have you placed nonskid appliques under movable items (i.e. rocking chair runners)? This keeps them in place.
☐	☐	Is the floor free of lamp cords? (Hint: Install a dimmer switch or have a flashlight within reach.)

Changing Table Safety

- Do not place toiletries on low shelves where they are inaccessible to you but handy to toddlers (both your own and visitors).

- Do not place toiletries on overhead shelves where they can fall inadvertently onto baby.

- Suspend supplies in hanging baskets from the ceiling or bolt organizers and shelves onto the wall within arm's reach.

- Use S-hooks and shower curtain rings to attach toys, pacifiers and manicure scissors onto shelves or baskets.

- Use a plastic doll for practice bathing and changing session. This "dry run" will allow you to organize all needed items within easy reach of the changing table.

- If you fear holding a slippery baby, purchase a pair of rubber gloves.

- Create mini-changing stations throughout the house. Place all needed items (i.e. diapers, baby wipes, changing pad, burp cloth, powder or lotion) in an easy-to-grab carrier such as a bucket or box.

Safety Evaluator

Yes	No	Consideration
		Fire
☐	☐	Do you have smoke detectors on each floor?
☐	☐	Do you have a battery-powered smoke detector in case the fire burns out your electric smoke detector?
☐	☐	Are smoke detectors in working order?
		When were they last checked? _____
☐	☐	Is the nursery identified from the outside by a safety sticker? The decals are available from fire fighters in your community.
☐	☐	Do you have a planned exit?
☐	☐	Is someone responsible for trying to reach the baby?
		Who? _____
		Mobiles
☐	☐	Is the rod strong enough to support the turning mechanism and the mobile's suspended pieces?
☐	☐	Is the rod securely fastened to the mobile unit?
		(Usually the rod connects to the musical works.)
☐	☐	Is the mobile unit fastened securely to the crib?
☐	☐	Are the pieces safe?
☐	☐	Are the pieces lightweight?
☐	☐	Do the pieces have rounded corners?

☐ ☐ Are the pieces well constructed? (Are notions such as eyes and bows firmly attached?)

☐ ☐ Can the mobile be fastened safely onto structures other than the crib (i.e. bassinet, perambulator, play yard and stroller)?

☐ ☐ Can the components be played with separately after the baby has outgrown the mobile?

☐ ☐ Can the components be changed or removed without destroying the mobile?

Car seat

☐ ☐ Do the straps appear to be comfortable (do not cut or bind)?

☐ ☐ Is the car seat made to accommodate a newborn?

☐ ☐ Are straps and buckles kept to a minimum without sacrificing safety?

☐ ☐ Are most metal parts mounted away from baby? (Metal parts can be heated in the sun and burn baby's skin.)

☐ ☐ Is the car seat anchored to the car according to the manufacturer's recommendations?

☐ ☐ Do you have a towel or blanket in the car to cover the car seat when not in use? This will shield any metal parts from the sun's rays.

☐ ☐ Is the car seat easy to clean?

☐ ☐ Is the car seat portable? (This is particularly important if you intend to use it in more than one car.)

☐ ☐ Can the car seat double as an infant carrier?

Nursery Floor Plan Organizer

After you have purchased your baby equipment, you must create a furniture floor plan. This simple organizer allows you to visualize several combinations without moving anything heavier than a piece of paper.

1. Measure your room carefully and plot the size of your nursery on the grid paper (page 57) with the following scale: 1 square equals 6 inches (2 squares equal one foot).

2. Mark all windows, doors, cold air returns and heat registers on the room outline.

3. Pencil in all features such as closet doors and built-in bookcases.

4. Mark all electrical outlets.

5. Trace the following page and cut out the pieces of furniture you intend to use in your nursery. If your equipment differs in size or is not provided, draw the pieces to scale from the graph paper.

6. "Move" the furniture about the room with the following suggestions in mind:

- Consider placing the crib and changing table along inside walls where the temperature is more constant.
- Do not place the crib or changing table in a draft created by windows or heating/cooling ducts.
- Allow ample clearance from walls and electrical wires for such items as rocking chairs, swings and circulating mobiles.

Nursery Floor Plan

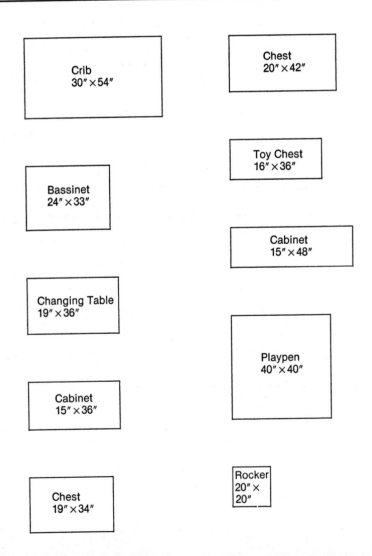

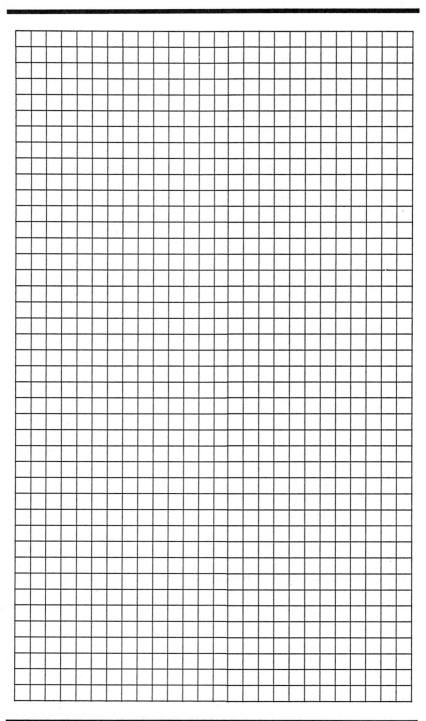

Chapter Five
Family Members and Household Needs

Preparing Siblings for Baby's Arrival

The timing and manner in which you announce the new baby's arrival depends upon a combination of age, development and other factors.

Time to Tell the Sibling

- When he or she is fearful that Mommy is sick. (This is especially important if your child is sensitive to your vomiting, faintness or mood swings.)
- When you begin to show your pregnancy. (Explain that Mommy is not getting fat.)
- Before another person inadvertently tells your child.
- After the first trimester, when the danger of a miscarriage has passed.
- After you make any of the following changes in your older child's routine:

    Potty training

    Moving into a bed from a crib

    Moving into another bedroom

    Moving into a booster seat from the high chair

    Moving into a co-pilot car seat from an infant car seat

    Enrolling in a nursery school or play group
- After you have moved into larger living quarters

Life With a Newborn and Sibling

- Focus attention on the older child.

- When visitors arrive with gifts have the older child help unwrap the gifts and give him or her a small gift or treat for being such a helpful big brother or sister.

- Preplan the difficult cranky periods, feeding times and bedtime. Write out a list of quiet activities to occupy the older child during these times:

    Read stories

    Listen to records and tapes

    Color

    Coordinate with favorite television program

    Tape child's favorite television program on a VCR

    Play favorite games

    List toys your child likes to play with alone.

    _____

    _____

    _____

    _____

    _____

    _____

    _____

    _____

Household Management

At the very time of your life when you least want to think about cleaning house—and, have little energy for doing it—a messy house can assume great importance. Guard against becoming over-whelmed by a new baby and a disorganized household. Preplan chores, activities and schedules. A system can help avoid arguments.

This section provides helpful information for the smooth running of your household. It tells whoever is taking over these chores where equipment is stored and what needs to be done, while saving you from having to manage all the details.

Equipment Checklist

Note the location within your house of all equipment and supplies. Write detailed instructions for all major appliances. Tape these instructions onto the equipment, being sure to include all idiosyncrasies such as odd sounds, shakes or hesitations. Check the list below for all equipment which can be found in your home.

Instructions written:

☐ washer	☐ dryer
☐ water softener	☐ air cleaner
☐ furnace/thermostat	☐ air conditioner
☐ water pump	☐ sump pump
☐ dehumidifier	☐ humidifier
☐ coffee maker	☐ grill
☐ stove	☐ microwave
☐ toaster oven	☐ ice maker
☐ dishwasher	☐ trash compactor
☐ garbage disposal	☐ snow blower
☐ lawn mower	☐ grass trimmer
☐ VCR	☐ television
☐ clock radio	☐ stereo
☐ answering machine	☐ programmed telephone
☐ vacuum cleaner	☐ electric broom
☐ floor waxer/polisher	☐ swimming pool filter/compressor
☐ timers	☐ _____
	☐ _____

Helper's Locator

Take a moment to note the location of the following household items. This information can save time and embarrassment because a helper will not need to search through closets and drawers.

Item	Location
Cleanup	
Broom	_____
Dust pan	_____
Mop/bucket	_____
All-purpose cleaners	_____
Floor cleaners	_____

Floor wax _____

Disinfectants _____

Sponges/rags _____

Paper towels _____

Trash bags _____

Light bulbs _____

Safety

Flashlights _____

Matches _____

Candles _____

First-aid Supplies _____

Laundry

Soap/softener/bleach/
spot removers _____

Iron _____

Ironing board _____

Starch _____

Medication

Vitamins _____

Special medications
(and directions for use) _____

Sundries

Toothpaste _____

Dental floss/
toothbrushes/mouthwash _____

Bubble bath _____

Shampoo/hair
conditioners _____

Combs/brushes _____

Sibling(s)

Special toy/blanket _____

Favorite book _____

Boots, gloves, hat _____

Sweaters, coat _____

School materials _____

Linens

Towels _____

Sheets _____

Extra blankets _____

Stationery supplies

Envelopes/writing paper _____
Stamps _____
Scissors _____
Scotch tape _____
Rubber bands _____
Stapler _____

Outdoor equipment

Lawn mower _____
Grass trimmer _____
Garden equipment _____
Rakes _____
Snow shovels _____
Outdoor toys _____
Bicycles _____

Pet supplies

Food _____
Grooming aids _____
Medications _____
Leash _____
Toys _____
Clean up _____

Emergency help

List individuals who can come to your aid in an emergency. This list can include craftsmen as well as close friends who you know will "come running."

Category	Name	Number
Handyman		
Plumber		
Helpful neighbor		
Close friend		
Relative		

Duty Roster

Is there one chore that drives you crazy if left unattended? Perhaps it is dirty dishes in the sink or newspapers strewn about the living room. Chances are those "little things" will become major during postpartum. Guard against such emotional time bombs by preplanning. Consider hiring a neighborhood kid to mow the lawn or weed the garden. Remember, your husband will be tired, too. Negotiate the following household duty roster between family members and friends who have volunteered to help.

Chore	Frequency	Person Responsible
Do laundry		
Take out garbage		
Wash dishes		
Do grocery shopping		
Prepare dinner		
Pay bills		
Run errands		
Dust		
Pick up newspapers/mail		
Clean bathroom		
Sweep floors		
Vacuum floors		
Wash floors		
Clean mirrors		
Pick up clothes		
Mow lawn		
Shovel snow		
Weed garden		
Gas up car		
Wash car		
Play with other children		
Other		

Family and Household Scheduler

Because you do not know when or for how long you will be in the hospital, take a moment to list the activities which will be occurring within your household. Be sure to include the time and location. (A map would be handy for helpers who are from out of town). A large wall calendar in a focal point of the house would be wise. The following events should be listed on your calendar:

Family members

Music lessons _____

Dance lessons _____

School hours _____

Car pools _____

(Try to have another mother cover for you. If this is impossible be sure you include a detailed map of each stop.)

Sporting events for which you have tickets _____

Club meetings _____

Parties _____

(Stock up on birthday party gifts in case your child gets an unexpected invitation.)

Special events _____

Religious schedules _____

(Include time and location of services for out-of-town guests.)

Household schedules

Pet schedule _____

(Feeding and walking schedules should be listed.)

Garbage pickup _____

(Note the procedure used—trash can vs. bags, time of pickup, location of pickup and any special instructions.)

Mail delivery _____

Deliveries _____

(This includes the milkman, UPS and retail deliveries.)

Shopping Organizer

"Be prepared" should be a new mother's motto. Stock up on the following items before the baby arrives:

To Buy	On Hand	Item
Laundry		
□	□	Laundry soap (including low-alkali laundry soap for the baby's clothes)
□	□	Prewash and spot remover
□	□	Bleach
□	□	Baking soda
□	□	Lemon juice
□	□	Ammonia
□	□	Fabric softener
□	□	Clothespins
Cleanup		
□	□	Floor cleaner and wax
□	□	Furniture polish
□	□	Glass cleaner
□	□	Bathroom cleaner
□	□	Dishwashing liquid/automatic dishwasher soap
□	□	Toilet paper
□	□	Tissues
□	□	Paper towels
□	□	Garbage bags (Many moms are surprised at the quantity of garbage generated. Remember you will be disposing of pads, diapers and wrapping paper.)
□	□	Vacuum bags and belts
□	□	Air fresheners/scented candles
□	□	Deodorant cakes for diaper pail
Food items		
□	□	Disposable plates, cups, eating utensils
□	□	Disposable aluminum casserole dishes
□	□	Paper napkins
□	□	Food wrap for leftovers
□	□	Fruits, juices, high-fiber foods (to combat constipation)
□	□	Beverages: soda, tea, decaffeinated coffee (especially needed by nursing mother)
□	□	Special treats for siblings (to reward positive behavior)
□	□	Pet food
□	□	Frozen sandwiches and pizza

Grocery List

Maintain a two-week supply of staples for your family and visiting guests. Consider stocking up on the following non-perishable items:

To Buy	On Hand	Item
Grains		
☐	☐	Bread
☐	☐	Pasta
☐	☐	Cereal
☐	☐	Crackers
☐	☐	Rice
☐	☐	Noodles
Quick meals		
☐	☐	Peanut butter
☐	☐	Soups
☐	☐	Canned tuna
☐	☐	Canned salmon
☐	☐	Canned chicken
☐	☐	Macaroni & cheese
☐	☐	Canned pasta
☐	☐	Pizza mix
☐	☐	Boxed processed cheese
☐	☐	Meals in a box (just add tuna, etc.)
Frozen/powdered items		
☐	☐	Milk
☐	☐	Breakfast mixes
☐	☐	Orange juice mixes
☐	☐	Bakery mixes
☐	☐	Coffee, tea
☐	☐	Drink mixes
Miscellaneous items		
☐	☐	Jelly
☐	☐	Relish
☐	☐	Condiments
☐	☐	Margarine
☐	☐	Eggs
☐	☐	Sugar
☐	☐	Jell-O
☐	☐	Canned fruit

Menu Planner

Write a suggested menu for out-of-town helpers. Be sure to indicate children's likes and dislikes as well as the dining routine.

	Menu	Location of Food	Preparation and Routine
Day 1			
Breakfast	_____	_____	_____
	_____	_____	_____
Lunch	_____	_____	_____
	_____	_____	_____
Dinner	_____	_____	_____
	_____	_____	_____
Day 2			
Breakfast	_____	_____	_____
	_____	_____	_____
Lunch	_____	_____	_____
	_____	_____	_____
Dinner	_____	_____	_____
	_____	_____	_____
Day 3			
Breakfast	_____	_____	_____
	_____	_____	_____
Lunch	_____	_____	_____
	_____	_____	_____
Dinner	_____	_____	_____
	_____	_____	_____
Day 4			
Breakfast	_____	_____	_____
	_____	_____	_____
Lunch	_____	_____	_____
	_____	_____	_____
Dinner	_____	_____	_____
	_____	_____	_____
Day 5			
Breakfast	_____	_____	_____
	_____	_____	_____
Lunch	_____	_____	_____
	_____	_____	_____
Dinner	_____	_____	_____
	_____	_____	_____

Some additional ideas

- Save fast-food restaurant coupons, especially from restaurants which are on your husband's way home from work or very near your home.
- During the last weeks of your pregnancy, double any casserole recipe which you serve your family and freeze the second casserole.
- Accept contributions from friends.
- Make a list of foods sold at the deli section of your grocery store.
- Compile a list of businesses which deliver. Establish credit or check privileges before the baby is born so that you need not worry about having the exact amount of cash.
- Have small amounts of cash available for helpers to run to the store.

Coupons

Shopping for postpartum is the ideal time to use coupons. During postpartum you will be buying more convenience foods and many baby items such as diapers, baby oil and baby food on a continuous basis. The benefits of couponing are twofold: significant savings and easier shopping for a friend or husband who might not be familiar with baby supplies. All the shopper has to do is find the item which matches the coupon. Friends and family can help you collect the appropriate coupons. On a larger scale, elicit the help of your fellow workers. Address envelopes with a short notice and leave them in an employee community area such as a lounge, bulletin board or cafeteria.

Sample notices

- I work in (department) and am having a baby in (month). Any baby coupons for items such as disposable diapers, bottles, baby toiletries, medicines or food would be greatly appreciated.
- My daughter (sister) is having a baby in (month). Being a practical future grandmother (aunt), I am collecting baby coupons. If you find any coupons for baby food, medicines, toiletries or disposable diapers, please donate them to the cause.

Chapter Six
Financial Planning

Examining Your Budget

The addition of a new family member can stretch a household budget from several directions. The additional expenditures for health care, baby clothing and equipment combine with loss of income if the mother is a wage earner. Examine your current budget with the help of our planner.

Anticipating Monthly Revenues

The answers to the following questions will help you determine your anticipated monthly revenues immediately after the baby arrives.

Yes	No	Consideration
		What is the last day you intend to work before the birth? _____
☐	☐	Are you returning to work after the birth? If so, what date do you plan to return to work? _____

If you are not planning to return to work:

Yes	No	Consideration
☐	☐	Will you be compensated for unused sick days?
☐	☐	Will you continue to receive benefits by using your vacation days first and then terminating employment as opposed to terminating employment on the last day of the job? (Benefits can include insurance, employee discounts, etc.)
☐	☐	Do you have maternity leave?
		If so, what is the length of coverage? _____
		What percentage of your monthly income is covered? _____
☐	☐	Does your husband have paternity leave?
		If so, what is the length of coverage? _____
		What percentage of his monthly income is covered? _____
☐	☐	Will your income fluctuate?
		If so, when will your income decrease? _____
		At what percentage? _____
☐	☐	Will your insurance coverage fluctuate?
		If so, when will your coverage terminate? _____

Monthly Income Statement

Complete this monthly financial analysis for each month of your pregnancy as well as for those months immediately after the baby is born.

Month	*Source* Father's Job	Mother's Job	Investments*	Other**	Monthly Total
1	_____	_____	_____	_____	_____
2	_____	_____	_____	_____	_____
3	_____	_____	_____	_____	_____
4	_____	_____	_____	_____	_____
5	_____	_____	_____	_____	_____
6	_____	_____	_____	_____	_____
7	_____	_____	_____	_____	_____
8	_____	_____	_____	_____	_____
9	_____	_____	_____	_____	_____
10	_____	_____	_____	_____	_____
11	_____	_____	_____	_____	_____
12	_____	_____	_____	_____	_____

*Include monthly interest and dividend payments which will be disbursed before the baby arrives and other anticipated monthly revenues.

**Include any money received from second jobs, consulting work, sale of handicrafts or outside financial support.

Monthly Expense Statement

Begin this process by examining your checkbook, bank card billing and other records of expenditures. Complete the form for the previous month and try to formulate a budget for the future. Expenditures that might increase with your new family addition are noted in the second column.

Fixed expenses

Item	Amount	Possible Changes
Rent/mortgage	_____	Larger living quarters
Auto payment	_____	

Insurance		Will change if mother
auto	————————	does not intend to return to work and her benefits in the past covered these insurance needs.
dental	————————	
health	————————	
home/property	————————	
life	————————	
Installment payments	————————	Likely to increase if you are charging baby expenses such as furniture, equipment and clothing.
Taxes	————————	Taxes will decrease with the addition of a new dependent. If you are purchasing major baby items, such as furniture, keep a record of sales taxes paid to reduce your tax liability at the end of the fiscal year.
Utilities	————————	Increased laundry needs.
Telephone	————————	Long-distance phone calls to talk about the baby.
TOTAL	————————	

Discretionary expenses

Item	Amount	Possible Changes
Auto		Commuting costs might increase if you move.
gas/maintenance	————————	
car pool costs	————————	
public transportation	————————	
Charitable contributions	————————	
Child care	————————	
Clothing	————————	Maternity and baby clothing
dry cleaning	————————	
Education	————————	
fees	————————	Classes, seminars
books and magazines	————————	
Entertainment	————————	
records and tapes	————————	
film rentals	————————	
Fitness and beauty	————————	
Food	————————	
Gifts and flowers	————————	

Home

Furniture	——————————	Baby's nursery.
Moving	——————————	If a move into larger quarters is necessary, plan to move early in the pregnancy to allow ample time to organize before the baby arrives.
Repairs	——————————	
Servicing	——————————	
Investments	——————————	
Savings	——————————	
Medical costs	——————————	Generally, well-baby visits are not covered by insurance companies.

Pocket money	
Allowance	——————————
Coffee money	——————————
TOTAL	——————————

Monthly Income / Expense Chart

Combine the information from the Monthly Income Statement with the information budgeted in the Monthly Expense Statement on the chart below.

Month	Income	Expenses	Surplus (deficit)
January	——————————	——————————	——————————
February	——————————	——————————	——————————
March	——————————	——————————	——————————
April	——————————	——————————	——————————
May	——————————	——————————	——————————
June	——————————	——————————	——————————
July	——————————	——————————	——————————
August	——————————	——————————	——————————
September	——————————	——————————	——————————
October	——————————	——————————	——————————
November	——————————	——————————	——————————
December	——————————	——————————	——————————
TOTAL	——————————	——————————	——————————

Motherhood Employment Checklist

Balancing motherhood and career is more complicated than the frequently asked question, "Are you coming back to work after the baby is born?" The checklist below offers suggestions for employment plus other details to be considered.

Returning to work full-time

• Arrange for child care.

• Arrange back-up child care for days when the baby is ill or the babysitter is unable to watch your child.

• Investigate employer's attitude toward time missed due to doctor's appointments, child's illness, etc.

• Reserve sick and vacation days to take time off when an emergency arises.

• If you intend to nurse, make arrangements for expressing milk. These arrangements should include:

> time

> quiet and private place

> refrigeration for storage

> pump and storage materials

Returning to work part-time

Investigate the following part-time options:

• substitute or back-up employment

• working less conventional hours such as weekends or evenings

• flex time

• job sharing

The mother choosing not to return to work

Consider those jobs which can be done from your home:

• free-lance editorial or art work

• market research/information retrieval

• computer programming

• office paperwork such as typing or bookkeeping

• child care (especially if you want your child to be around other children)

• elder care (caring for an older person)

• consulting work

• expansion of domestic duties such as laundry, sewing, cooking and baking

• handicrafts sold to consignment stores

Insurance and Investment Information

It's very important to have all your records in order and to know who to consult with your investment and insurance questions. The following charts will help you get all this material organized.

Insurance Information Form

Company name: _____
Policy number: _____ ⟨ _____
Effective: _____
Member's name: _____
Social Security number: _____

Deductible amounts

Family deductible: _____
Individual deductible: _____
For mother: _____
For baby*: _____
*(Will charges of the last three months of the year carry over into the new year's deductible?)

Additional information

Account number: _____
Plan code: _____
Benefit codes: _____
Telephone information: _____

In addition to the information above, you should know the answers to the following commonly asked questions concerning your maternity benefits.

Yes	No	Question
☐	☐	Does the policy have any "pre-existing" conditions?
☐	☐	Does the policy allow me to select my physician and hospital or must I use only those affiliated with my health maintenance organization?
☐	☐	Is there a "reasonable and customary" clause in the policy? (This means that the policy will cover only those fees which are considered average for your community. If your physician submits a bill that is three times that of a comparable physician's services, your insurance will not cover the inflated amount.)
		Who is responsible for the paperwork (documenting costs, filing, etc.)? _____
		How will payment be made? Will the insurance company pay the physician, midwife, hospital, etc., directly?_____

Individual who answered my questions: _____
Date: _____
Verified by correspondence dated: _____
(attach all correspondence)

Health Care Cost Planner

Avoid unnecessary costs by learning what your insurance policy will and will
not pay. Experienced maternity patients quickly learn how to submit bills and
request services in the "language" of their insurance policy. Evaluate your
coverage and plan for your maternity costs by using the following checklist.

Maternal care

Services	Item Covered Yes	No	At What Percentage	Contingent Upon
Physician's fees	☐	☐	_____	_____
Obstetrical				
Pre-natal visits	☐	☐	_____	_____
Vaginal delivery	☐	☐	_____	_____
Cesarean delivery	☐	☐	_____	_____
In-hospital visits	☐	☐	_____	_____
Phone consultations	☐	☐	_____	_____
Postpartum checkup	☐	☐	_____	_____
Anesthesiologist	☐	☐	_____	_____
Family practice physicians	☐	☐	_____	_____
Consulting physicians	☐	☐	_____	_____
High-risk pregnancy	☐	☐	_____	_____
Midwife's fee	☐	☐	_____	_____
Certified Nurse Midwife	☐	☐	_____	_____
Labor coach	☐	☐	_____	_____
Nursing	☐	☐	_____	_____
Private	☐	☐	_____	_____
Staff	☐	☐	_____	_____
Nursing care at home	☐	☐	_____	_____
Genetic counseling	☐	☐	_____	_____
Dental care	☐	☐	_____	_____

Classes

    Prenatal ☐ ☐ _____ _____

    Exercise ☐ ☐ _____ _____

    Nutrition ☐ ☐ _____ _____

    Breastfeeding ☐ ☐ _____ _____

    First aid ☐ ☐ _____ _____

    Baby care ☐ ☐ _____ _____

Medication

In-hospital prescribed ☐ ☐ _____ _____

In-hospital administered ☐ ☐ _____ _____

Outpatient ☐ ☐ _____ _____

Under physician's care ☐ ☐ _____ _____

Under midwife's care ☐ ☐ _____ _____

Anesthesia

    Caudal ☐ ☐ _____ _____

    Epidural ☐ ☐ _____ _____

    Spinal ☐ ☐ _____ _____

    Saddle ☐ ☐ _____ _____

    Pudendal ☐ ☐ _____ _____

    Paracervical ☐ ☐ _____ _____

    Local ☐ ☐ _____ _____

Intravenous fluids (I.V.) ☐ ☐ _____ _____

Supplies

Sanitary pads ☐ ☐ _____ _____

Nursing pump and pads ☐ ☐ _____ _____

Sitz bath ☐ ☐ _____ _____

Egg shell mattress ☐ ☐ _____ _____

"Doughnut" for
hemorrhoids ☐ ☐ _____ _____

Procedures

Pregnancy test

    At-home ☐ ☐ _____ _____

    Physician's office ☐ ☐ _____ _____

Sonogram ☐ ☐ _____ _____

Amniocentesis ☐ ☐ _____ _____

Stress/nonstress tests ☐ ☐ _____ _____

Fetal heart monitoring ☐ ☐ _____ _____

Lab work

    Blood workup ☐ ☐ _____ _____

    Variety of titers ☐ ☐ _____ _____

    Genetic testing ☐ ☐ _____ _____

    Toxoplasmosis test ☐ ☐ _____ _____

Newborn Care

	Item Covered			
	Yes	No	At What Percentage	Contingent Upon
Services				
Length of coverage				
Baby covered at birth:				
If well?	☐	☐	_____	_____
If ill?	☐	☐	_____	_____
Nursery supplies				
Bottles	☐	☐	_____	_____
Diapers	☐	☐	_____	_____
Medication	☐	☐	_____	_____
Circumcision tray	☐	☐	_____	_____
Special nursery supplies				
Incubators	☐	☐	_____	_____
Oxygen	☐	☐	_____	_____
I.V.	☐	☐	_____	_____
Medication	☐	☐	_____	_____
Monitors	☐	☐	_____	_____
Physician's fees				
Pediatrician				
Initial interview	☐	☐	_____	_____
In-hospital visits	☐	☐	_____	_____
In-hospital examinations	☐	☐	_____	_____
Consulting physicians	☐	☐	_____	_____
Well-baby visits	☐	☐	_____	_____
Immunizations	☐	☐	_____	_____

Hospital costs

	Item Covered			
	Yes	No	At What Percentage	Contingent Upon
Rooms				
Emergency room	☐	☐	_____	_____
Labor room	☐	☐	_____	_____
Birthing room	☐	☐	_____	_____
Operating room	☐	☐	_____	_____
Recovery room	☐	☐	_____	_____
Patient				
Private	☐	☐	_____	_____
Semi-private	☐	☐	_____	_____
Telephone	☐	☐	_____	_____
Television	☐	☐	_____	_____
Board				
Patient's meals	☐	☐	_____	_____
Guest trays (husband's)	☐	☐	_____	_____

Knowledge of your policy's "fine print" can save you money. Essentially any condition or criteria which has been established by the insurance company before payment can be disbursed will be listed. Plus, any deductible amount, any procedure which must be ordered only by the physician or activity which must occur in the hospital to be covered by the policy will be listed.

For example, if your physician orders a breast pump for you while in the hospital, it might be covered. If you purchase a breast pump yourself, it might not be covered. Examine your policy carefully.

Professionals To Consult About Baby's Future

Professional	Purpose

□ **Attorney**

Writing wills, trusts, etc.

Name: _____
Address: _____
Phone: _____
Location of important papers (such as
wills): _____

□ **Accountant**

Financial and tax liability information

Name: _____
Address: _____
Phone: _____
Location of important papers (such as
tax returns): _____

□ **Broker**

Investment counseling

Name: _____
Address: _____
Phone: _____
Location of important papers (such as
stock certificates): _____

□ **Estate Planner**

(See also: Attorney)

Name: _____
Address: _____
Phone: _____
Executor of your estate: _____

□ **Insurance Agent**

Name: _____
Address: _____
Phone: _____
Location of important papers (such as
policies): _____
Health policy name: _____
Policy number: _____
Life policy name: _____
Policy number: _____

Mother and Father Fact Sheet

This information might be necessary at a later date when your child applies for a passport, benefits, etc. If you have died, the information might not be easily available to the guardian. Therefore, complete the form and keep it in a safe place.

Information	Mother	Father
Full name:	_____	_____
Date of birth:	_____	_____
Place of birth:		
City:	_____	_____
County:	_____	_____
State (or country):	_____	_____
Social Security number:	_____	_____
Mother's full name:		
(baby's grandmother)	_____	_____
Date of birth:	_____	_____
Place of birth:	_____	_____
Father's full name:		
(baby's grandfather)	_____	_____
Date of birth:	_____	_____
Place of birth:	_____	_____
Past employment:		
• Name of company:	_____	_____
Address:	_____	_____
Period of employment:	_____	_____
• Name of company:	_____	_____
Address:	_____	_____
Period of employment:	_____	_____
• Name of company:	_____	_____
Address:	_____	_____
Period of employment:	_____	_____
Insurance policies:		
• Health policy name:	_____	_____
Health policy number:	_____	_____
• Life policy name:	_____	_____
Life policy number:	_____	_____
• Auto policy name:	_____	_____
Auto policy number:	_____	_____
Pensions:		
Name of company:	_____	_____
Address:	_____	_____

Investments:
- Type of investment: _____ _____
  Name of company: _____ _____
  Address: _____ _____
- Type of investment: _____ _____
  Name of company: _____ _____
  Address: _____ _____
- Type of investment: _____ _____
  Name of company: _____ _____
  Address: _____ _____

Family heirlooms:
- Type of heirloom: _____ _____
  Location: _____ _____
  Significance: _____ _____
  Approximate value: _____ _____
- Type of heirloom: _____ _____
  Location: _____ _____
  Significance: _____ _____
  Approximate value: _____ _____
- Type of heirloom: _____ _____
  Location: _____ _____
  Significance: _____ _____
  Approximate value: _____ _____

Baby's Financial Future—Social Security Card

A Social Security number is now required for all accounts which draw interest. You can give your Social Security number for a child's savings account or you can apply for a Social Security card for the baby. Follow the checklist below to obtain a Social Security card for your child.

Obtaining a Social Security Card

☐ Complete Social Security Administration Form #5 available from the Social Security Administration in person or through the mail.

☐ Present two forms of identification. These must be originals; for example, crib card, birth certificate and immunization records.

☐ Take the above to the Social Security office, usually located in the Federal Building, or mail it to the Social Security office. If you mail the originals, the material will be returned within 10 days. The card and number take approximately four to eight weeks to process.

84

List of Baby's Investments

Record all securities and investments purchased for your child. This is important if the investments are intended to be long term. Your child may encounter difficulty computing tax liability when he or she sells the securities 25 years from the date they were purchased.

Name of Security	Purchase Price	Number of Shares	Date Purchased

Savings account:
  Name of bank: _____
  Account Number: _____

Chapter Seven
Celebrations

Baby Showers

You will not be planning your own baby shower, of course, out your input is important so the hostess knows what you really need, what day is best, and who to invite.

Shower Planner

Host/Hostess: _____

"Women Only" or mixed couples: _____

Date: _____

Time: _____

Location: _____

Activities planned: _____

_____

_____

Menu/shower goodies (cake, punch, etc.): _____

_____

_____

_____

_____

_____

_____

Both expectant grandmothers (and grandfathers if the shower is mixed) should be invited.

Planning a date for a shower can be very tricky. Don't wait until the last two weeks as you might be in the hospital. One month prior to your due date is often an accepted date for a shower. Also, some mothers prefer to have the shower after the baby arrives.

Guests*

			R.S.V.P.	
Name	**Address**	**Phone**	**Yes**	**No**
_____	_____	_____	☐	☐
_____	_____	_____	☐	☐
_____	_____	_____	☐	☐
_____	_____	_____	☐	☐
_____	_____	_____	☐	☐
_____	_____	_____	☐	☐
_____	_____	_____	☐	☐
_____	_____	_____	☐	☐
_____	_____	_____	☐	☐
_____	_____	_____	☐	☐
_____	_____	_____	☐	☐
_____	_____	_____	☐	☐

*Be sure that the size of the guest list does not exceed the space available. Also, unlike your wedding shower, you might not be physically comfortable in a crowd of people.

Mother's Wish List

Clothing

Item	Number	Size
Cloth diapers	_____	_____
Waterproof pants	_____	_____
Gowns/kimonos	_____	_____
Sweater/bootie sets	_____	_____
Booties	_____	_____
Sun suit/diaper sets	_____	_____
Disposable diapers	_____	_____
Shirts	_____	_____
Stretch suits	_____	_____
Blanket sleeper	_____	_____
Bibs	_____	_____
Bunting	_____	_____
Socks	_____	_____

Linens

Item	Number	Color
Crib sheets		
Receiving blankets		
Washcloths		
Bath towels		
Infant seat cover		
Car seat cover		
Crib blankets		
Waterproof lap pads		
Hand towels		
Hooded bath towels		
Playpen cover		
High chair cover		

Baby supplies

- ☐ Diaper bag
- ☐ Digital thermometer
- ☐ Cool mist vaporizer
- ☐ Bottle set
- ☐ Grooming set (brush/comb)
- ☐ Pacifier
- ☐ Baby scales
- ☐ Blunt edge nail scissors
- ☐ Bottle sterilizer

Baby toys

- ☐ Mobile
- ☐ Stuffed animals
- ☐ Rattles
- ☐ Cloth books

Baby equipment

- ☐ Crib
- ☐ Playpen
- ☐ Night light
- ☐ Cradle
- ☐ Crib bumpers
- ☐ Port-a-crib
- ☐ Car seat
- ☐ Jumper/exerciser
- ☐ Infant backpack
- ☐ Changing table
- ☐ Bassinet
- ☐ Lamp
- ☐ Moses basket
- ☐ Infant seat
- ☐ Baby bath
- ☐ Diaper pail
- ☐ Walker
- ☐ Newborn front pack carrier

Books for mother's library

Title   **Author**

_____   _____
_____   _____
_____   _____
_____   _____
_____   _____

Additional information

Color of nursery: _____
Theme of nursery: _____
Services a friend could provide in lieu of a gift:
   ☐ Watch siblings
   ☐ Prepare a meal
   ☐ Grocery shop
   ☐ Clean the house
   ☐ Have the new family over for dinner
   ☐ Help finish a needlecraft project for the baby
   ☐ Install a dimmer switch in the nursery
   ☐ Assemble baby furniture/equipment
   ☐ Paint/wallpaper the nursery
   ☐ Help plan religious ceremony

Note: If you are in need of a more expensive item, suggest to your hostess that she advise guests to buy one group gift.

Baby's Gift List

Keep track of all gifts received for baby on this form.

Given by	Gift	When and Where Received	Thank You Sent
_____	_____	_____	☐
_____	_____	_____	☐
_____	_____	_____	☐
_____	_____	_____	☐
_____	_____	_____	☐
_____	_____	_____	☐
_____	_____	_____	☐
_____	_____	_____	☐
_____	_____	_____	☐
_____	_____	_____	☐
_____	_____	_____	☐
_____	_____	_____	☐
_____	_____	_____	☐
_____	_____	_____	☐
_____	_____	_____	☐
_____	_____	_____	☐
_____	_____	_____	☐
_____	_____	_____	☐
_____	_____	_____	☐
_____	_____	_____	☐

Advice on Motherhood and Child Care

There is something about pregnancy which causes friends, family and total strangers to feel free about offering suggestions. I think it is because you are too immobile to run away from them.

On the positive side, however, you will receive some excellent advice. The space below is provided to jot down the most noteworthy information. This can be an activity at your baby shower.

	From	**Advice Given**
Pregnancy	_____	_____
		_____
		_____
		_____
Birthing	_____	_____
		_____
		_____
		_____
Child Care	_____	_____
		_____
		_____
		_____
Dealing with Siblings	_____	_____
		_____
		_____
		_____
Household Hints	_____	_____
		_____
		_____
		_____
Babysitters	_____	_____
		_____
		_____
		_____

Religious Ceremonies

Careful planning and attention to detail will help you relax and enjoy the religious ceremony. Much of the planning can be done before baby arrives.

Planning a Religious Ceremony

☐ Contact officiant.

What are your obligations to church/temple? ———

_____

_____

	Yes	No
Are there time requirements which must be fulfilled?	☐	☐
Are you permitted to give input into the service?	☐	☐
Can you write any of the service?	☐	☐
Can you request particular music?	☐	☐
Can you request a particular celebrant or vocalist?	☐	☐
Where will the service be conducted? ————		
Are there seating limitations?	☐	☐
What is the maximum number of guests? ————		

☐ Determine and contact godparents (sponsors).

Be sure they are aware of their obligations and part in the ceremony, if any.

☐ Select christening gown or special outfit.

Wait until after the child is born to purchase a new gown, unless you are aware of the sex of the baby beforehand. If you are considering a family heirloom, be sure it fits and has been checked for yellowing.

☐ Make a guest list. (Use the following form to keep track of your guests and responses.)

Name	Address	Phone	R.S.V.P.* Yes	No
_____	_____	_____	☐	☐
_____	_____	_____	☐	☐
_____	_____	_____	☐	☐
_____	_____	_____	☐	☐
_____	_____	_____	☐	☐
_____	_____	_____	☐	☐
_____	_____	_____	☐	☐
_____	_____	_____	☐	☐
_____	_____	_____	☐	☐
_____	_____	_____	☐	☐
_____	_____	_____	☐	☐
_____	_____	_____	☐	☐

*Direct R.S.V.P.'s to a friend who volunteered to help. You don't want guests calling you when you return home with your newborn.

☐ Select invitations (pre-address them) or phone the guests.

☐ Determine if a party will follow the ceremony.

Location:

☐ Community hall at the church or temple

☐ At home (arrange for cleaning before the party, set up of tables and supplies, menu and clean-up after the party)

☐ Rented area

Menu:

☐ Cake/punch

☐ Snack trays (cheese, vegetables, fruits, hot/cold hors d'oeuvres)

Meal:

☐ Catered

☐ Prepared and frozen ahead of time

☐ Prepared and served by helpers not attending ceremony

Chapter Eight
Day Care and Babysitters

Day Care

A number of factors must be evaluated when choosing day care to provide for your baby's safety and your peace of mind.

Options and Resources

- ☐ Public subsidized day care
- ☐ Privately supported day care
- ☐ Church affiliated day care
- ☐ Child care at a babysitter's home:
    - ☐ Relative
    - ☐ Friend
    - ☐ Professional day care home provider
- ☐ In-house child care:
    - ☐ Housekeeper/child care giver
    - ☐ Relative
    - ☐ Student in exchange for room and board
    - ☐ Grandmother/grandfather
- ☐ Sources of information
    - ☐ Friends
    - ☐ Employer
    - ☐ Pediatrician
    - ☐ Church or temple
    - ☐ State licensing agencies
    - ☐ Newspaper advertisements
    - ☐ Local college or university personnel department
    - ☐ Foreign student exchange
    - ☐ Yellow Pages under "Child Care"

Child Care Information Form

Everyone gives the same two pieces of advice regarding finding child care: Check with friends and start looking now! Use the form below for recording information on child care.

Friend's name: _____

   Type of day care*: _____

   Caregiver's name: _____

   Phone: _____

   Cost per week: _____

   Evaluation of day care: _____

Friend's name: _____

   Type of day care: _____

   Caregiver's name: _____

   Phone: _____

   Cost per week: _____

   Evaluation of day care: _____

Friend's name: _____

   Type of day care: _____

   Caregiver's name: _____

   Phone: _____

   Cost per week: _____

   Evaluation of day care: _____

Friend's name: _____

   Type of day care: _____

   Caregiver's name: _____

   Phone: _____

   Cost per week: _____

   Evaluation of day dare: _____

*Public subsidized, privately supported or church-affiliated center or babysitter (in-house, out-of-house).

Child Care Evaluator

Health and safety

	Good	Fair	Poor
How clean is the facility/home?	☐	☐	☐
How frequently are the linens changed?			
_____	☐	☐	☐
How are they laundered? _____			
_____	☐	☐	☐
How are soiled diapers disposed? _____			
_____	☐	☐	☐
What is the cleaning schedule for the facility/home? _____	☐	☐	☐
Are the caregivers required to wash their hands after changing a baby? _____	☐	☐	☐
Are infants separated from older children?			
_____			
(Toddlers may inadvertently hurt a younger child.)	☐	☐	☐
Is there a workable evacuation plan in case of a fire or other disaster?	☐	☐	☐
Does the baby equipment comply with safety standards?	☐	☐	☐
Does the facility/babysitter refuse a sick child who is contagious?	☐	☐	☐
How many outbreaks of serious contagious illness did they have last year (other than colds)? _____	☐	☐	☐
Will the caregivers administer medication prescribed for your child? _____	☐	☐	☐
Is that information charted? _____	☐	☐	☐
Are physical examinations required before a child is accepted into the center?			
_____			
_____	☐	☐	☐
Are immunization records required? _____	☐	☐	☐
How are babies fed? _____	☐	☐	☐
How sanitary is the bottle preparation area?	☐	☐	☐

	Good	Fair	Poor
How secure is the child against child stealing?	☐	☐	☐
What are the procedures for another person—other than you or your husband—to pick up the child? _____ _____	☐	☐	☐
Are you free to enter and leave the facility at any time during working hours? _____	☐	☐	☐
Is the center overcrowded?	☐	☐	☐
Are the rooms adequately heated, air-conditioned, ventilated and lighted?	☐	☐	☐

Nurturing

	Good	Fair	Poor
What is the ratio of caregivers to infants? (One to two or three is very good with one to eight considered poor.)	☐	☐	☐
How consistent is the care?	☐	☐	☐
Can you request a particular caregiver for your child or are assignments impersonal in the day care? (Constancy of care is very important.)	☐	☐	☐
How stimulating is the environment?	☐	☐	☐
Is the room bright and cheery?	☐	☐	☐
Can you bring toys and mobiles from home to decorate the baby's crib?	☐	☐	☐
Are the babies rocked and put into infant seats or do they remain in their cribs most of the day?	☐	☐	☐
What is the noise level?	☐	☐	☐
Is there music in the background?	☐	☐	☐
What are the credentials of the staff/babysitter? (Include questions such as educational attainment, interests, experience, church or social affiliations. Look for a caregiver who gives genuine affection and shows an interest in your child.)	☐	☐	☐

Working operation

What are the hours? _____ ☐ ☐ ☐

How often was the center closed during
the past three years due to inclement
weather? _____
(A day care center which is unable to care
for your child can create havoc with your
work schedule.) ☐ ☐ ☐

What is the payment schedule? _____ ☐ ☐ ☐

Are you charged for the days you do not
bring your ill baby to the center? ☐ ☐ ☐

Will the center advise you of child care
tax credits? _____
(Such benefits are based on family
income and range from $1,400 per family
maximum to 30 percent of the child care
costs up to $2,400 for a family income of
$10,000 or less.) ☐ ☐ ☐

Does the babysitter report her income and
pay her own Social Security? (Beware of
the babysitter who doesn't want you to
file for your tax credit, and instead will
give you a discount on your child care.
She probably is not reporting the income
earned from babysitting.) ☐ ☐ ☐

Is the center/babysitter licensed by the
appropriate government agency? _____
(In most states the requirements are
minimal so do not consider a license to
be an endorsement.) ☐ ☐ ☐

Are you responsible for disposable
diapers, formula, etc.? _____ ☐ ☐ ☐
(Some day care centers require canned
formula which is more expensive than
powdered.) ☐ ☐ ☐

Will the center accept frozen breast milk?

_____ ☐ ☐ ☐

Will the babysitter/caregiver ever be taking
your child out of the house/center?

_____ ☐ ☐ ☐

Other considerations

Does the babysitter have animals in the house? _____	☐	☐	☐
Are they separated from the baby? _____	☐	☐	☐
If the babysitter is coming into your home, does he/she have private or public transportation to your home? _____	☐	☐	☐
Who will assume the cost? _____	☐	☐	☐
Does the babysitter smoke? yes___ no ___			

Babysitters

It's vital for Mom and Dad to have a night out now and then. Start lining up babysitters before baby arrives. The competition for them is often stiff!

The Occasional Evening Out

Suggestions for finding a neighborhood teenager who babysits

- Ask mothers in the neighborhood.
- Stroll your baby by a school bus stop as the bus deposits the students. The potential babysitter will find you!
- Be observant. Watch teenagers strolling babies. They probably are either babysitters or older brothers and sisters.
- Advertise in your church bulletin, neighborhood newspapers, fliers, etc.
- Consult local schools' guidance departments.

Questions to ask

- Do you have experience with newborns?
- Have you taken an infant care class at a hospital or through a community service organization?
- Will you need a ride to and from your house?
- Will your parents be home? (A young babysitter feels more comfortable if she can call her mom for advice or help.)
- How much per hour do you charge?

List of Babysitters

Name of sitter	Phone Number	Performance Rating	Comments
_____	_____	_____	_____
_____	_____	_____	_____
_____	_____	_____	_____
_____	_____	_____	_____
_____	_____	_____	_____

Babysitter's Information Organizer

Phone numbers

Where we will be: _____

Number where we can be reached: _____

Emergency number for immediate assistance: _____

Physician (name): _____

(number): _____

Poison Control number: _____

Neighbor who can help (name): _____

(number): _____

Police: _____

Fire: _____

Baby's schedule

Feeding: _____ ounces of _____ at_____ am/pm

_____ ounces of _____ at_____ am/pm

_____ ounces of _____ at_____ am/pm

Location of bottles: _____

Location of nipples: _____

Preparation instructions: _____

Location of bibs: _____

Location of burp cloths: _____

Special feeding instructions: _____

Changing

Location of clean diapers: _____
Disposal of soiled diapers: _____
Supplies needed to clean baby: _____
Special changing instructions: _____

Location of clean clothing: _____

Activity, sleeping

Put to sleep at/after: _____
Special instructions:
   Special blanket/toy/diaper: _____
   Special music/mobile: _____
   Lights: _____
   Requires rocking/singing: _____
   Do not allow to cry for more than: _____

To comfort

☐ Place in infant seat
☐ Rock
☐ Pacifier
☐ Sing
☐ Turn on stereo
☐ Take for a walk
   Location of stroller: _____
☐ Place in infant pouch
   Location of pouch: _____
☐ Burp
☐ Read story
☐ Turn on intrauterine sound effects
☐ _____
☐ _____
☐ _____

Always keep the following two forms in the diaper bag:

Emergency Information List

Mother's name: _____

   Mother's office phone: _____

Father's name: _____

   Father's office phone: _____

Home phone: _____

Home address: _____

Directions for getting to home in case of emergency: _____

Emergency number for immediate assistance: _____

Physician's name: _____

   Physician's phone: _____

   Hospital affiliation: _____

   Hospital phone: _____

In an emergency, contact:

- Name: _____
  Phone: _____
- Name: _____
  Phone: _____
- Name: _____
  Phone: _____
- Police: _____
- Fire: _____

Child's Allergies: _____

Additional information: _____

Medical Release Form

The emergency room of _____ Hospital has my permission to treat my child, _____ , for any immediate care needed. Our insurance company is _____ and the policy number is _____ .

_____

Signature

_____

Date

Chapter Nine
Final Countdown

Your bag is packed, sibling care is planned, and you know how to get to the hospital. The following checklists will speed you on your way with the knowledge that you are truly organized!

Sibling Care Organizer

Before labor begins

☐ Notify day care of alternate people picking up child

☐ Notify school of alternate people picking up child

If labor begins during the day at home

☐ Call (name): _____ at (phone): _____
who expects to:

    ☐ Pick up your child at the house

    ☐ Pick up your child at school

    ☐ Call school (phone): _____

    ☐ Come over to the house

    ☐ Have you drop the child off at her/his house

    ☐ Other plans: _____

If labor begins during the day while at work

☐ Call day care (phone): _____

☐ Call (name): _____ at (phone): _____
who expects to:

    ☐ Pick up your child at the babysitter's

    ☐ Pick up your child at day care

    ☐ Come to your house and pick up the child

    ☐ Have you drop the child off at her/his house

    ☐ Other plans: _____

If labor begins at night

☐ Call (name): _____ at (phone): _____
who expects to:
- ☐ Pick up your child at your house and return to his/her house
- ☐ Wait at home for you to drop off child
- ☐ Come over and spend the night at your house
- ☐ Other plans: _____
_____

If sibling will be sleeping overnight away from home

- Consider sleepovers before the baby's birth.
- Discuss what to expect (i.e. waking up in another bed, different routine and menu at mealtime, wearing clothes packed in the suitcase and different daily schedules).
- Discuss how many nights your child can expect to sleep overnight.

Prepare a checklist for your child's suitcase

- ☐ Favorite blanket or stuffed toy
- ☐ Small variety of other favorite toys, books, etc.
- ☐ Picture of Mommy and Daddy
- ☐ Pajamas (two pair)
- ☐ Several changes of clothing
- ☐ Diapers, if needed

Items to Take to the Hospital

Coach's bag

- ☐ Camera/film/flash (Consider an instant camera so that pictures can be shown immediately, especially to an anxious older brother or sister.)
- ☐ Tape recorder and tapes to tape the birth or send tapes home to a sibling.
- ☐ Focal point
- ☐ Washcloth
- ☐ Rolling pin or tennis ball for back labor
- ☐ Lip balm
- ☐ Lollipops
- ☐ High-protein snacks

- ☐ Stop watch
- ☐ Paper/pencil for record keeping
- ☐ Magazine or book
- ☐ List of important phone numbers

Mother's suitcase

- ☐ Going-home outfit (Don't expect miracles. Pack a loose-fitting style.)
- ☐ 2-4 nightgowns (Select gowns of natural fibers which will be comfortable next to baby's skin. Avoid synthetic fabrics; it can be difficult enough getting comfortable without doing battle with a slippery nightgown. If you intend to nurse, select gowns which allow easy access or p.j.s with full tops and bottoms.)
- ☐ Robe (Bring a robe which opens completely; it may be difficult to step into or pull a zipper-style robe over your head.)
- ☐ Slip-on slippers or thongs (Waterproof thongs have the dual advantage of being usable in the shower.)
- ☐ 2-4 bras (If you intend to nurse, purchase nursing bras the last month of your pregnancy. Otherwise, bring tightly fitting bras.)
- ☐ 4-6 underpants (Pack maternity and regular underpants. A tighter fitting underpant may feel more comfortable.)
- ☐ Sundries:
    - ☐ Toothpaste
    - ☐ Toothbrush
    - ☐ Shampoo
    - ☐ Comb and brush
    - ☐ Make-up
    - ☐ Deodorant
    - ☐ Perfume (Some hospitals allow you to place a drop of perfume on the bassinet for the baby to smell.)
    - ☐ Chapstick
- ☐ Watch
- ☐ Birth announcements (Address and stamp the envelopes before the baby arrives.)
- ☐ Stationery and thank-you notes (See thank-you notes in this section.)
- ☐ Address book with telephone numbers and addresses
- ☐ Long-distance telephone credit card
- ☐ Credit card number (Makes shopping easier if you want to send a gift to a special friend.)
- ☐ Small photograph of your other children (Allow the sibling to help you pack his or her picture. Also be sure it is visible when he comes to visit.)
- ☐ Small gifts for siblings at home

Baby's clothing

- ☐ 2 outfits (Pack one for each sex with the intention of returning the inappropriate outfit. Many hospitals take a picture of your newborn and will dress the baby in the outfit which you bring. Otherwise, the baby will be dressed in a hospital T-shirt.)
- ☐ Hat/bonnet
- ☐ Blanket
- ☐ Bunting if baby is due during the cooler seasons. (The bunting should have a crotch so the seat belt in the child's car seat can be fastened.)
- ☐ Booties/shoes with socks

Paperwork

- ☐ Insurance information form (or insurance card) or the following information:

  Name of the company which holds the policy: _____

  Policy number: _____

  Effective dates: _____

  Member's name: _____

  Social Security number: _____

  Additional information on card:

      Plan code: _____

      Benefit code: _____

- ☐ Pre-registration forms or other information requested from the hospital.
- ☐ Telephone numbers:

  Back-up for sibling care: _____

  Telephone numbers of sibling's school or day care: _____

  _____

  Back-up for work: _____

  Telephone number for husband: _____

  Persons who should be notified that you are in labor: _____

  _____

  Family: _____

  Close friend: _____

Personal Belongings Inventory

Many hospitals request an inventory of valuable belongings brought to the hospital. Because you will want to leave your room, do not take anything that will tempt a thief. This check-list will help you keep track of your belongings. Make a copy for the hospital staff to put in your chart.

Patient's name: ————————— Room number: —————————

Coach's bag contents:

- ☐ Camera/film/flash
- ☐ Focal point
- ☐ Rolling pin/tennis ball
- ☐ Lollipops
- ☐ Stop watch
- ☐ Book/magazine

- ☐ Tape recorder and tapes
- ☐ Washcloth
- ☐ Lip balm
- ☐ High-protein snacks
- ☐ Paper/pencil
- ☐ List of phone numbers

Suitcase contents:

☐ Jewelry: ———————————————————————

☐ Clothing worn when you entered the hospital: ————————

☐ Going-home outfit: ——————————————————

- ☐ Nightgowns
     Number: ——————————
- ☐ Slippers
- ☐ Panties
     Number: ——————————
- ☐ Stationery
- ☐ Credit cards
- ☐ Money
- ☐ Baby's clothing: ——————————

- ☐ Robe
- ☐ Bras
     Number: ——————————
- ☐ Stamps
- ☐ Address book
- ☐ Long-distance credit card number
- ☐ Wallet
- ☐ Sundries

☐ Other: ———————————————————————

Hospital Route Planner

This planner can be used for your trip to the hospital or to give directions to out-of-town guests. Be sure to include street names, number of traffic lights, landmarks and mileage. Draw a map on the back for additional information.

Directions if trip is during rush hour:

From home to the hospital: _____

_____

Approximate time: _____

From work to the hospital: _____

_____

Approximate time: _____

Directions if trip is during off-hours:

From home to the hospital: _____

_____

Approximate time: _____

From work to the hospital: _____

Approximate time: _____

Use this space to sketch out a map of the hospital route.

Early Labor Record

Complete this record before entering hospital or clinic.

Obstetrician's phone:
   Day: _____
   Evening: _____
Time to call obstetrician: _____
Instructions given by obstetrician: _____

Time	Contraction Interval	Notation
_____	_____	_____
_____	_____	_____
_____	_____	_____
_____	_____	_____
_____	_____	_____
_____	_____	_____
_____	_____	_____
_____	_____	_____
_____	_____	_____
_____	_____	_____
_____	_____	_____

Additional symptoms:

Symptom	Time
☐ Passing of mucus plug	_____
☐ Rupturing of the membranes	_____
☐ Nausea/indigestion	_____
☐ Spurt of energy	_____

Comfort techniques:

- Warm shower
- Napping
- Walking
- Rocking on hands and knees
- Breathing techniques

What to Do in the Hospital

Hospitals can be very boring places, especially when your baby is asleep. Consider the following activities:

- Sleeping, followed by napping, followed by dozing off, followed by resting, followed by snoozing.
- Admiring baby
- Participating in hospital-sponsored child care classes
- Mailing birth announcements
- Phoning friends and family. It is particularly important to call home and speak with siblings. Make the conversations short and frequent.
- Reading
- Doing needlecraft
- Writing thank-you notes (see page 112)
- Being comfortable! Be advised of the following postpartum measures which are available to make you more comfortable. Because some of them require a doctor's order, request them during his or her rounds.
  - shower/wash hair
  - egg-crate mattress
  - laxatives/stool softeners
  - analgesics—pain killers
  - sedatives—for sleep and to relieve anxiety
  - perineal care—analgesics for episiotomy
    pre-moistened towelettes
    sitz bath
    heat lamp
    ice packs
  - breast care—nursing:
    cream for nipples
    nipple shield
  - non-nursing breast care:
    binder
    ice bags
    medication to decrease lactation

"Favors" to Ask from Friends

Care for sibling

Names: _____

_____

Check up on the care of sibling (stop in to see if all is well).

Names: _____

_____

Save the newspaper on the date of the baby's birth

Names: _____

_____

Bring in your mail and newspaper

Name: _____

Care for the family pet

Instructions: _____

_____

Name: _____

Telephone other friends with the good news

Telephone tree: _____

_____

Pick up printed birth announcements

Name: _____

Help with religious ceremony (see pages 91-92)

Names: _____

_____

_____

Last minute errands

Names: _____

_____

How To Thank Your Helpers

Don't forget to thank your helpers. Consider the following list of ideas, which not only show your appreciation, but also give your new family a chance to be alone. During the early adjustment period, many new parents (and grandparents) need "space." Plan time outs for your helpers who will probably welcome the chance to get out of the house. Be sure to draw a detailed map, if your helpers are unfamiliar with the city.

Thank you ideas

- Theater tickets—Many theaters take ticket orders over the phone and will charge them to a major credit card.

- Movie tickets—Purchase gift certificate tickets ahead of time at the theater.

- Dinner reservations—Purchase a gift certificate or call the restaurant and make arrangements to have the bill sent to you.

- Friends—Arrange an evening out with mutual friends. Perhaps a friend who has volunteered to help could have your guests over for dinner or cocktails.

- Tourist ideas—Prepare a list of local tourist activities or special events occurring in your city. Prepurchase tickets when possible.

Sample Thank-You Notes

Dear _____,

How thoughtful of you to help us celebrate (baby's name) arrival. The (flowers/balloons) are so beautiful and certainly add that special touch to a very happy occasion. Thank you.

I can't believe that our little (prince/princess) has arrived. However, he/she reminds me frequently with a good bellow. You will have to hear (baby's name) in person very soon.

Thanks again,

Dear _____,

What a pleasant surprise to return to my room and find the lovely flowers. (Baby's name) stares at the bright colors and I enjoy their cheerfulness. Thank you for thinking of us.

(Husband's name) and I are getting acquainted with (baby's name). It was love at first sight . . . and sound! He/she has (husband's name) (eyes/ears) and my (hair/fingers). You will have to see for yourself soon.

Love,

Dear _____,

It was so nice of you to take the time to (visit/call/send a note). Of course, (husband's name) and I never tire of bragging about (baby's name). He/she is truly _____ lbs. _____ ozs. of joy.

(Baby's name) certainly is lucky to have been born into a circle with (family/friends) like yourself who show such concern. Thank you.

Love,

Dear _____,

What a thoughtful gift! How did you know that we needed a (gift item) for (baby's name)? Only you would have been so clever. The (gift item) is perfect.

Speaking of perfect, let me tell you about (baby's name). He/she was born (date or day) weighing _____ lbs. and _____ ozs. His/her eyes are (color) and he/she has (color and amount) hair. Of course, (husband's name) and I see various family traits such as my (eyes/ears) and his (nose/hair). A photo will be forthcoming.

Thank you,

Dear _____,

(Baby's name) (will look or looks, depending on the size) adorable in the precious outfit which you sent him/her. The color is perfect and he/she will wear it in good health. Thank you for your thoughtfulness.

I am looking forward to getting into a routine with (baby's name). It is hard to believe that he/she is here. That is, until (baby's name) reminds us with a smile.

Sincerely,

Items to Take Home from the Hospital

Did you know that almost everything you use in the hospital is yours to take home? Check with the nurse, but generally the following items are your property:

Mother's property

- Any opened medication
- Plastic sitz bath
- Inflatable rings for hemorrhoids
- Surgical stockings or footies
- Nursing pads

- Egg-crate mattress
- Soap dishes
- Disposable pillow
- Breast pump
- Sanitary supplies

Baby's supplies

- Any opened medication
- Unopened bottles of formula or water

- Disposable diapers
- Pacifier

Hint: Many a mother has hoarded the disposable formula and water bottles. They are very convenient when you have returned home and do not have the time or energy to fix a bottle. Collect the bottles by simply taking them out of the bassinet each time the baby is given one. However, in the event that the nursery is keeping track of the baby's intake, you should notify them of what you are doing.

Also, take the crib card and any other documentation of baby's birth. This is very important for obtaining a Social Security card.

Leaving the Hospital Checklist

☐ Request a cart for father to take flowers, gifts and suitcases down to the car beforehand.

☐ Check out in the business office.

☐ Arrange for an infant car seat and have it in the center of the back seat.

☐ Allow sibling to come to the hospital.

☐ Request no visitors at home.

☐ Unplug the telephones at home.

Pediatrician's Instructions

Feeding instructions: _____
_____
_____
_____
_____
_____

Sleeping patterns: _____
_____
_____
_____
_____
_____

Review of medication: _____
_____
_____
_____
_____
_____

Other special care: _____
_____
_____
_____
_____
_____

Pediatrician's name: _____
Pediatrician's office phone: _____
Office hours: _____
Home phone: _____

Resources

Books and Magazines

Magazines

American Baby, 575 Lexington Avenue, New York, NY 10022. (212) 752-0775. Monthly; for expecting parents through those of one-year-olds.

Baby Talk, 185 Madison Avenue, New York, NY 10016. (212) 679-4400. Monthly; for expecting parents through those of two-year-olds.

Growing Child, 22 North Second Street, Lafayette, IN 47902. (317) 423-2624. Monthly; for parents of newborns through those of six-year-olds.

Mothers Today, 441 Lexington Avenue, New York, NY 10017. (212) 867-4820. Bimonthly; for expecting parents through those of four-year-olds.

Mothering, Box 2208, Albuquerque, NM 87103. (505) 867-3110. Quarterly; for parents of newborns through those of five-year-olds, though some articles cover older children.

Parents Magazine, 685 Third Avenue, New York, NY 10017. (212) 878-8700. Monthly; for expecting parents through those of pre-teenagers.

Pediatrics for Parents, 176 Mount Hope Avenue, Bangor, ME 04401. (207) 942-6212. Monthly; for expecting parents through those of teenagers.

Practical Parenting Newsletter, 18326B Minnetonka Boulevard, Deephaven, MN 55391. (612) 475-1505. Bimonthly; for expecting parents through those of pre-schoolers.

Twins Magazine, P.O. Box 12045, Overland Park, KS 66212. (800) 821-5533. Bimonthly; the only national magazine for the parents of twins.

Working Mother, 230 Park Avenue, New York, NY 10169. (212) 551-9412. Monthly; for parents of infants through pre-schoolers.

Books

Baby care

Kelly, Paula, M.D. *First Year Baby Care* (Meadowbrook)
Spock, Benjamin, M.D. *Baby & Child Care* (Pocket Books).

Child development

Brazelton, T. Berry. *Infants and Mothers* (Delacorte).
Caplan, Frank. *The First 12 Months of Life* (Bantam).
Hagstrom, Julie and Joan Morrill. *Games Babies Play* (A&W Visual Library).
Lansky, Bruce. *Baby Talk* (Meadowbrook).
Levy, Dr. Janine. *The Baby Exercise Book* (Pantheon).

Parenting

Kelly, Marguerite and Elia S. Parsons. *Mother's Almanac* (Doubleday).
Lansky, Vicki. *Dear Babysitter* (Meadowbrook).
—*Practical Parenting Tips* (Meadowbrook).
Sullivan, S. Adams. *Father's Almanac* (Doubleday).

Pregnancy

Cooke, Courtney. *The Best Baby Shower Book* (Meadowbrook).
Lansky, Bruce. *The Best Baby Name Book* (Meadowbrook).
Regnier, Susan. *Exercises for Baby & Me* (Meadowbrook).
Simkin, Penny, Janet Whalley and Ann Keppler. *Pregnancy, Childbirth and the Newborn* (Meadowbrook).

Grandparenting

Sicora, Jean. *Handbook for Beginning Grandparents.* (R.C. Press).

Food and nutrition

Dana, Nancy and Anne Price. *Successful Breastfeeding* (Meadowbrook).
La Leche League. *The Womanly Art of Breastfeeding* (La Leche League).
Lansky, Vicki. *Feed Me! I'm Yours* (Meadowbrook).

Medical care

Hart, M.D., Terril H. *The Parent's Guide to Baby and Child Medical Care* (Meadowbrook).
Pantell, M.D., Robert H. et al, *Taking Care of Your Child* (Addison Wesley).

Humor

Barry, Dave. *Babies and Other Hazards of Sex* (Rodale Press).
Johnston, Lynn. *David, We're Pregnant!* (Meadowbrook).
—*Hi Mom! Hi Dad!* (Meadowbrook).
—*Do They Every Grow Up?* (Meadowbrook).
Lansky, Bruce. *Mother Murphy's Law* (Meadowbrook).

National Organizations

Birth defects and genetic abnormalities

March of Dimes Birth Defects Foundation
1275 Mamaroneck Avenue
White Plains, NY 10605

National Easter Seal Society, Inc.
2023 W. Ogden Street
Chicago, IL 60612

National Genetics Foundation, Inc.
555 West 57th Street
New York, NY 10019

General child care

American Academy of Pediatrics
Office of Public Education
1801 Hinman Avenue
Evanston, IL 60206

Day Care and Child Development Council of America, Inc.
1012 14th Street N.W.
Washington, D.C. 20005

La Leche League International (breastfeeding)
9616 Minneapolis Avenue
Franklin Park, IL 60131

U.S. Consumer Product Safety Commission
1750 K Street N.W.
Washington, D.C. 20207

U.S. Department of Health, Education and Welfare
Public Health Service
5600 Fishers Lane
Rockville, MD 20852

Superintendent of Documents
U.S. Government Printing Office
Washington, D.C. 20420

Family life

North American Council on Adoptable Children
2001 S Street N.W., Suite 540
Washington, D.C. 20009

Parents Without Partners
7910 Woodmont Avenue
Bethesda, MD 20814

Stepfamily Association of America
28 Allegheny Avenue, Suite 1307
Baltimore, MD 21204

The Step Family Foundation, Inc.
333 West End Avenue
New York, NY 10023

Special concerns (Caesarean)

Caesarean Way
128 Jefferson Street
Riverside, NJ 08075

Childbirth at home

Association for Childbirth at Home
P.O. Box 1219
Cerritos, CA 90701

Multiple births

The Center for Study of Multiple Birth
333 East Superior Street, Suite 463-5
Chicago, IL 60611

Death

Compassionate Friends, Inc.
Box 1347
Oak Brook, IL 60521

National SIDS Foundation
2 Metro Plaza, Suite 205
8240 Professional Place
Landover, MD 20785

Nutrients and Vitamins*

Key Nutrient	RDA	Functions	Sources	Comments
Calories	N —1,800 - 2,100 P —2,100 - 2,400 L —2,300 - 2,600	• Provides energy for tissue building and increased metabolic requirements.	Carbohydrates, fats, proteins	Calorie requirements vary according to your size, activity level and weight.
Water, liquids	N —4 cups P —8+ cups L —8+ cups	• Carries nutrients to cells. • Carries waste products away. • Provides fluid for increased blood and amniotic fluid volume. • Helps regulate body temperature. • Aids digestion.	Water, juices, milk	Often neglected, but is an important nutrient.
Protein	N —46g P —76 - 100g L —66g	• Builds and repairs tissues. • Helps build blood, amniotic fluid and placenta. • Helps form antibodies. • Supplies energy.	Meat, fish, poultry, eggs, milk, cheese, dried beans, dried peas, peanut butter, nuts, whole grains, cereals	Fetal requirements increase by about 1/3 in late pregnancy as the baby grows.
Minerals				
Calcium	N —800 mg P —1,200 mg L —1,200 mg	• Helps build bones and teeth. • Important in blood clotting. • Helps regulate use of other minerals in your body.	Milk, cheese, whole grains, vegetables, egg yolk, canned fish, ice cream	Fetal requirements increase in late pregnancy.

Phosphorus	N —800 mg P —1,200 mg L —1,200 mg	• Helps build bones and teeth.	Milk, cheese, lean meats	Calcium and phosphorus exist in a constant ratio in the blood. An excess of either limits use of calcium.
Iron	N —18 mg P —18+ mg L —18+ mg	• Combines with protein to make hemoglobin. • Provides iron for fetal storage.	Liver, red meats, egg yolk, whole grains, leafy vegetables, nuts, legumes, dried fruits, prunes, prune juice, apple juice	Fetal requirements increase tenfold in last 6 weeks of pregnancy. Supplement of 30 to 60 mg of iron daily is recommended by the National Research Council.
Zinc	N —15 mg P —20 mg L —25 mg	• Component of insulin. • Important in growth of skeleton and nervous system.	Meat, liver, eggs, seafood, especially oysters	Deficiency can cause fetal malformations of skeleton and nervous system.
Iodine	N —150 mcg P —175 mcg L —200 mcg	• Helps control the rate of body's energy use. • Important in thyroxine production.	Seafoods, iodized salt	Deficiency may produce goiter in infant
Magnesium	N —300 mg P —450 mg L —450 mg	• Coenzyme in energy and protein metabolism. • Enzyme acivator. • Helps tissue growth, cell metabolism and muscle action	Nuts, cocoa, green vegetables, whole grains, dried beans, dried peas	Most is stored in bones. Deficiency may cause neuromuscular dysfunctions.

Fat soluble vitamins

Vitamin A	N —4,000 IU P —5,000 IU L —6,000 IU	• Helps bone and tissue growth and cell development. • Essential in development of enamel-forming cells in gum tissue. • Helps maintain health of skin and mucous membranes.	Butter, fortified margarine, green and yellow vegetables, liver	In excessive amounts, it is toxic to the fetus. It can be lost with exposure to light.

Vitamin D	N —200 - 400 IU P —400 - 600 IU L —400 - 600 IU	• Needed for absorption of calcium and phosphorus, as well as mineralization of bones and teeth.	Fortified milk, fortified margarine, fish liver oils, sunlight on your skin	Toxic to fetus in excessive amounts. Is a stable vitamin.
Vitamin E	N —12 IU P —15 IU L —15 IU	• Needed for tissue growth, cell wall integrity, and red blood cell integrity.	Vegetable oils, cereals, meat, eggs, milk, nuts, seeds	Enhances absorption of vitamin A.

Water soluble vitamins

Folic Acid	N —400 mcg P —800 mcg L —600 mcg	• Needed for hemoglobin synthesis. • Involved in DNA and RNA synthesis. • Coenzyme in synthesis of amino acids.	Liver, leafy green vegetables, yeast	Deficiency leads to anemia. Can be destroyed in cooking and storage. Supplement of 400 mcg per day for pregnant women is recommended by the National Research Council. Oral contraception use may reduce serum level of folic acid.
Niacin	N —13 mg P —15 mg L —17 - 20 mg	• Coenzyme in energy and protein metabolism.	Pork, organ meats, peanuts, beans, peas, enriched grains	Stable; only small amounts are lost in food preparation.
Riboflavin (B2)	N —1.2 mg P —1.5 mg L —1.7 - 1.8 mg	• Coenzyme in energy and protein metabolism	Milk, lean meat, enriched grains, cheese, leafy greens	Severe deficiencies lead to reduced growth and congenital malformations. Oral contraception use may reduce serum concentration of riboflavin.
Thiamin (B1)	N —1.1 mg P —1.5 mg L —1.6 mg	• Coenzyme for energy metabolism.	Pork, beef, liver, whole grains, legumes	Its availability limits the rate at which energy from glucose is produced.
Pyridoxine (B6)	N —2.0 mg P —2.5 mg L —2.5 mg	• Important in amino acid metabolism and protein synthesis. • Fetus requires more for growth.	Unprocessed cereals, grains, wheat germ, bran, nuts, seeds, legumes, corn	Excessive amounts may reduce milk supply in lactating women. May help control nausea in early pregnancy.

Cobalamin (B12)	N —3.0 mcg P —4.0 mcg L —4.0 mcg	• Coenzyme in protein metabolism. • Important in formation of red blood cells.	Milk, eggs, meat, liver, cheese	Deficiency leads to anemia and central nervous system damage. Is manufactured by micro-organisms in intestinal tract. Oral contraception use may reduce serum concentrates.
Vitamin C	N —60 mg P —80 mg L —60 mg	• Helps tissue formation and integrity. • Is the "cement" substance in connective and vascular substances. • Increases iron absorption.	Citrus fruits, berries, melons, tomatoes, chili peppers, green vegetables, potatoes	Large doses in pregnancy may create a larger-than-normal need in infant. Benefits of large doses in preventing colds have not been confirmed.

Be sure to read the labels on the food you buy. This information can help you choose the right foods for your family. Labels with nutritional information tell you what you are getting for your money and give you the information you need to plan a well-balanced diet.

N—nonpregnant
P—pregnant
L—lactating

*The main source for information in this chart is *Nutrition in Pregnancy and Lactation* eds. B. Worthington-Roberts, J. Vermeersch, and S. Williams (St. Louis: C.V. Mosby Co., 1981).

Pregnancy, Childbirth and the Newborn
by Simkin, Whalley, and Keppler

The Childbirth Education Association of Seattle's illustrated guide to nutrition, health, exercise, labor, birth, breastfeeding, and new baby care is the most widely used prenatal training text in America.

Order #1169

Baby & Child Medical Care
edited by Terril H. Hart, M.D.

Here's the fastest source of baby medical information. It contains the most authoritative information, with treatments for over 150 common children's illnesses, injuries, and emergencies. Includes a symptoms index.

Order #1159

First-Year Baby Care
by Paula Kelly, M.D.

This handbook covers the first twelve months of life—when parents need help most! The step-by-step photos and illustrations make the up-to-date, authoritative information easy to use. This book covers bathing, diapering, feeding, first aid, child-proofing, and more.

Order #1119

Baby & Child Emergency First Aid Handbook
by Mitchell J. Einzig, M.D.

The next best thing to 911, this user-friendly book has a quick-reference index on both covers, large illustrations and easy-to-read instructions on the most common childhood emergencies, and a durable hard cover that lays flat.

Order #1380

Order Form

Qty.	Title	Author	Order No.	Unit Cost	Total
	Baby & Child Emergency First Aid	Einzig, M.	1380	$15.00	
	Baby & Child Medical Care	Hart, T.	1159	$8.00	
	Baby Talk	Lansky, B.	1039	$3.95	
	Best Baby Name Book	Lansky, B.	1029	$5.00	
	Best Baby Shower Book	Cooke, C.	1239	$7.00	
	David, We're Pregnant!	Johnston, L.	1049	$6.00	
	Discipline Without Shouting/Spanking	Wyckoff/Unell	1079	$6.00	
	Do They Ever Grow Up?	Johnston, L.	1089	$6.00	
	Feed Me! I'm Yours	Lansky, V.	1109	$9.00	
	First-Year Baby Care	Kelly, P.	1119	$7.00	
	Funny Side of Parenthood	Lansky, B.	4015	$6.00	
	Getting Organized for Your New Baby	Bard, M.	1229	$5.00	
	If We'd Wanted Quiet/Poems for Parents	Lansky, B.	3505	$12.00	
	Joy of Parenthood	Blaustone, J.	3500	$6.00	
	My First Years Record Book		3129	$15.00	
	Our Baby's First Year Calendar		3179	$10.00	
	Pregnancy, Childbirth, and the Newborn	Simkin/Whalley/Keppler	1169	$12.00	
	Practical Parenting Tips	Lansky, V.	1179	$7.00	
	Working Woman's Guide to Breastfeeding	Dana/Price	1259	$7.00	
				Subtotal	
				Shipping & Handling (see below)	
				MN residents add 6.5% sales tax	
				Total	

YES! Please send me the books indicated above. Add $2.00 shipping and handling for the first book and 50¢ for each additional book. Add $2.50 to total for books shipped to Canada. Overseas postage will be billed. Allow up to 4 weeks for delivery. Send check or money order payable to Meadowbrook Press. No cash or C.O.D's, please. Prices subject to change without notice. **Quantity discounts available upon request.**

Send book(s) to:

Name _____ Address _____

City _____ State _____ Zip _____

Telephone (_____)_____ P.O. number (if necessary) _____

Payment via: ❑ Check or money order payable to Meadowbrook Press (No cash or C.O.D.'s, please)

Amount enclosed $ _____ ❑ Visa (for orders over $10.00 only.)

❑ MasterCard (for orders over $10.00 only.)

Account # _____ Signature _____ Exp. Date _____

A *FREE* Meadowbrook Press catalog is available upon request.
You can also phone us for orders of $10.00 or more at 1-800-338-2232.

Mail to: Meadowbrook, Inc.
18318 Minnetonka Boulevard, Deephaven, MN 55391
(612) 473-5400   Toll -Free 1-800-338-2232   Fax (612) 475-0736